Thomas Jefferson

THE CONTINUING AMERICAN REVOLUTION

Odie B. Faulk & Billy M. Jones

ARCHER EDITIONS PRESS

Library of Congress Cataloging in Publication Data

Faulk, Odie B.

Miracle of the Wilderness

Bibliography: P. Index
SUMMARY: Traces the evolution and implementation of
the concept of equal rights from the Revolution to the
present.
1. Civil rights—United States—History. [1. Civil
rights—History] I. Jones, Billy M., joint author.
II. Title.
JC599.U5F36   323.4'0973   76-57766
ISBN 0-89097-010-6

MIRACLE OF THE WILDERNESS

All pictures used in this book are from the Library of Congress.

CONTENTS

For SEYMOUR V. CONNOR

In Appreciation, Friendship, and Respect

Preface

The people of the United States have just completed celebrating—with great enthusiasm—the bi-centennial of the Declaration of Independence which heralded the birth of the nation. Each state, city, local organization, and individual marked the occasion in its own way with little national direction. Some Americans criticized the federal government for not sponsoring "official" bi-centennial events, believing that the two-hundredth anniversary of the Declaration of Independence should have been marked by some national ceremony. However, the method employed more properly fitted the philosophical basis of the nation. "We the people" is a phrase running throughout the Declaration, the Constitution, and the Bill of Rights, for the founding fathers firmly believed that governments were instituted by the citizens themselves; thus it was fitting that celebrations of the birth of the nation were at the individual and local level.

And every American, whatever his race or creed or color or date of entry of him (or his ancestors) into the country had something to celebrate. A majority of the citizens of this country did not have ancestors fighting in the small, outnumbered Continental Army of General George Washington. Far fewer present-day Blacks, Orientals, Latin Americans, and Indians had forefathers participating in those battles or in the deliberations of the Continental Congress or Constitutional Convention. Moreover, none of us today can shed blood retroactively in the fight of those patriots two hundred years ago, thereby making ourselves one with the founders of the country.

However, no present American must have had ancestors fighting in 1776 or deliberating in Philadelphia in order to be a part of the American Revolution, for that revolution is still taking place. The Declaration of Independence stated a basic belief in the rights of individuals and in their power to create governments which served their needs. The Constitution did just that: it established a government to serve the needs of the American people. The Bill of Rights was added almost immediately to restate the ideals of the Declaration of Independence. In the years since 1791, change has come through legislation and constitutional amendment— peacefully, quietly, and legally. There was no need to overthrow the government by revolution, for revolution had been institutionalized so that change could come without bloodshed and bullets. Thus any American who believes in these ideals and who works to secure desirable changes through constitutional means himself becomes a part of the on-going American Revolution.

This book is not an attempt to write a definitive history of the revolutionary era of the United States. Many learned studies have been done covering the Declaration of Independence, the Constitution, the Bill of Rights, and the individuals involved in each of these events. Rather the authors attempt herein to trace the evolution and implementation of an idea and an ideal—that all men have natural rights and that governments exist only to secure those rights to individuals. This idea was stated first by Greek and Roman philosophers, then surfaced again during the Renaissance and the Reformation, and was given strong voice during the Age of the Enlightenment. The idea gained practical experience during those years when America was nothing more than a few British colonies along the eastern seaboard; it grew into imperfect reality during the frustrations of separation from England; it was institutionalized in permanent form as the founding fathers sought to establish a more perfect union; and it has evolved into more concrete form as each succeeding generation has rededicated itself to the idea. Our goal was to trace this thread—this steel hawser—from its conception through the formative years of the republic to the present; in the process we hoped to show that almost every major facet of American history relates to this idea and this ideal. By so doing, we hoped to explain the true essence of America.

In writing this book the authors have incurred numerous debts. Specifically we wish to thank the members of the Memphis Bi-Centennial Commission, who conceived this as a project they wished to sponsor: Howard Willey, Chairman; Mrs. Wells Awsumb, Vice-Chairman; P. K. Seidman, Vice-Chairman; Stanley Huggins, Secretary; and Mac Holladay, Executive Director. And librarians at Oklahoma State University and Memphis State University aided in the search for documents. In addition, we wish to thank the many scholars who have contributed monographic and documentary details of this era; their pioneering made our task much easier. Finally we thank Professors Seymour V. Connor, Carl Tyson, and James Smallwood for their suggestions, and Kathy Powers for typing the manuscript.

Odie B. Faulk

Billy M. Jones

Miracle of The Wilderness

There was surprisingly little unity among the thirteen colonies engaged in a war with mighty England in June of 1776. Few people anywhere had a sense of nationhood or of unity. Those living in the South and the Mid-Atlantic states disliked and distrusted New Englanders. Militiamen from one colony would refuse to fight outside the borders of their territory. Other Americans believed the entire struggle to be wrong and wanted to restore harmony with the crown. And everywhere there was unrest, for people realized the old order was giving way to something new and unknown.

Sitting in the parlor of rented rooms in Philadelphia, Thomas Jefferson faced the difficult task of finding words to bring unity and purpose to Americans, to give voice to "an expression of the American mind," and to couch these words in "the proper tone and spirit called for by the occasion." His was a task virtually impossible, for nothing in his background indicated an identification with the common American. He was in his thirty-third year that June of 1776, an aristocratic Virginian so shy with strangers that he found it difficult to make an effective public speech. He had been educated by private tutors, attended William and Mary College, and studied law with George Wythe, one of the great lawyers of that day. His education had brought him fluency in several classical languages, a deep and abiding interest in science, and a thirst to know the thinking of social philosophers. He thus was lawyer, classicist, philosopher, and thinker, as well as musician, poet, and inventor—an impractical man whose plantation of Monticello rarely turned a profit because he was more interested in experiments than in raising yet another crop of tobacco.

Moreover, his domestic life was a source of great unhappiness to him in Philadelphia that warm summer of 1776. His wife Martha was so ill he feared she might die at any moment, as had their eighteen-month-old daughter the previous autumn. Through the spring of 1776 Jefferson had abandoned the Continental Congress to return home. There he had assumed her duties of running the household, as well as managing the plantation, spending his evenings reading favorite books to his fragile wife. Only the most urgent appeals from friends in the Congress had brought the red-haired, six-feet-tall Virginian back to Philadelphia. There his reputation for a "masterly pen" brought his appointment to the committee assigned to draft a declaration of independence.

Serving with him on that committee were John Adams, Benjamin Franklin, and two lesser-known Americans, Robert Livingston and Roger Sherman. Other than Jefferson, only Adams and Franklin were of sufficient stature to draft the document; however, Franklin had a son known to be sympathetic to England, while Adams was a New Englander suspect in the Southern and Middle-Atlantic colonies. Jefferson at first had proposed that Adams should write the declaration, but Adams had refused, saying, "You shall do it."

"Oh, No!" responded Jefferson.

Adams, remembering this incident years later, recalled the arguments he had used to persuade Jefferson: "Reason 1st. You are a Virginian and Virginia ought to appear at the head of this business. Reason 2nd. I am obnoxious, suspected and unpopular; you are very much otherwise. Reason 3rd. You can write ten times better than I can."

"Well," said Jefferson, "if you are decided I will do as well as I can."

Jefferson, after seeing Adams' version of how the first draft of the Declaration came to be written, differed. In 1823, in a letter to James Madison, the ex-President, then eighty years old, wrote that the full committee of five members, had met, whereupon "they unanimously pressed on myself alone to undertake the draught. I consented; I drew it...."

Once he agreed to write a first draft, Jefferson withdrew to the rooms he had rented on the corner of Market and Seventh streets in Philadelphia. These were on the second floor of a home owned by a young man named Graff, a bricklayer. Sitting down at a portable writing desk of his own invention, Jefferson had no books or pamphlets to which to turn for inspiration or ideas, for his library had been left behind at Monticello. Yet he had within his memory the aid of dozens of men who had given serious thought to questions of human liberty, of government, and of society.

Through reading, Jefferson had become familiar with the classical literature of Greece and Rome and could write knowingly of the ideas of Homer, Aristotle, Plato, Plutarch, Cicero, Horace, and Caesar. He understood that in this ancient period humans had sought maximum freedom, for he had read of early attempts at democracy in the ancient Greek city-state of Athens, just as he was familiar with the fundamental concepts behind the Roman republic. He knew, as did other colonial writers, of the virtues of simplicity, patriotism, and justice—and of the vices and corruption brought on by greed and a lust for power; he equated the former with the small, rustic beginnings of Greece and Rome and the latter with the tyranny of imperial Rome. Thus it was natural for him to see the American colonies as similar to the old-fashioned, simple days of the Greek city-state, just as he likewise compared England with the corruption of the latter days of the Roman empire when justice was bought and sold and the ordinary citizen had no protection of life and property.

Having more influence on Jefferson—and his contemporaries—than the history and writings of antiquity, however, were the more immediate events of the past three centuries: the Renaissance, the Reformation, and the Enlightenment. When the Roman Empire had collapsed on being invaded by barbarians, the political, economic, and intellectual techniques that had enabled both Greeks and Romans to govern themselves in large territorial units, with extensive foreign trade, were gradually lost. Small, self-sufficient, agriculturally oriented communities replaced the empires. Trade was reduced to a minimum, and government was effective only at the local level where there was a contractual agreement between lord and vassals. The vassal worked the land (or had his own vassals to do so), fought in the lord's army, and rendered judgment in the lord's court; in return he received protection and justice. Although there was a complicated system of rules designed to insure justice, the word of a strong lord usually prevailed. And a united league of strong lords could even impose their will on a king, as was the case with King John of England in 1215; when he persisted in punishing his vassals without trial and in raising money in ways the lords believed to be illegal, they forced him to sign the Great Charter in which he promised to cease these illegal practices.

Only one strong institution survived during this period as a unifying force throughout Europe: the Roman Catholic Church. Its control over the minds and ideas of men was strong in a society which glorified the afterlife and sought to please God. Because of this power, conflicts between popes and kings for political power were frequent.

Gradually, however, there began a change. As men traveled—on crusades or for trade—they became aware of a world outside their own localities, and they began to seek more knowledge about this world rather than the one to be experienced after death. This period of Renaissance (rebirth) was characterized by a renewed interest in knowledge—of the past, of this world, of man. As scholars studied the writings of the Greeks and Romans, they encountered scientific theories about the nature of the universe that sharply differed from the official view approved by the Church. Copernicus, a mathematician and astronomer, in the year 1530 published a short abstract arguing that the earth revolved around the sun and turned on its axis; his theory directly contradicted the approved theory of the Church, for had not Joshua caused the sun to stand still in the heavens. Because this new theory was heresy, the Church had it suppressed—but the damage had been done. Scientists refused to accept a return to the old order; where Copernicus had pioneered, others soon followed. Galileo with a telescope confirmed the Copernican theory, while Descartes, Bacon, Isaac Newton, and others advanced the frontiers of knowledge and logic. Science and the scientific method gradually replaced the Church as the final determinant of truth.

The leaders fought back, and from time to time they were able to suppress some of the new discoveries—but only briefly. Galileo was condemned and forced to recant, but science marched on. The new order could be seen in the contrasting attitudes of St. Augustine, who in the fourth century stated, *"I think. Therefore God is,"* and Descartes, a French philosopher of the eighteenth century who said, *"I think. Therefore I am."* Man was becoming humanistic. No longer could scientific truth be dictated and inflexible; it was subject to proof by laboratory experiment. Because the Church had refused to accept the new truth, scientists talked of discovering the laws of nature.

Where these scientists led, others followed. Change came in many directions. The Christian religion fragmented as the Reformation gained force, and feudalism faded as nations emerged with kings who claimed complete power by *"Divine Right"* (the theory that they received their power from God). According to this interpretation, to rebel against any king, good or bad, was to rebel against God's will.

As the Age of the Enlightenment emerged, political philosophers became disgusted with arbitrary political orthodoxy, just as had scientists with the orthodox doctrines of the Church. They began to wonder if there were natural laws governing societies just as natural law governed the physical universe—and to formulate any they might discern. In seeking these natural laws of society, they turned to man's distant past—to the age when man had lived in a state of nature and when he first attempted to institute a government.

Because of their Christian heritage, these political philosophers agreed that the world had begun in the Garden of Eden. In that age man had earned his bread (property) by the sweat of his brow. But too many men had been brutish and selfish and had taken by force the property—and sometimes the life and liberty—of other men. Therefore men in a state of nature, in order to live in harmony with each other, gradually had formed governments whose task it was to protect life, liberty, and property. During the centuries that followed, these governments had fallen into the hands of the few through the laws of inheritance, bringing to the throne kings who were corrupt and who arbitrarily took life, liberty, and property. The general will of the people had been subverted.

An even greater problem for social scientists of the seventeenth century, however, was to explain away a revolution that swept some king out of office. If that king had been placed on the throne by God, then the rebels, even if successful, were heretics—unless some new explanation could be formulated. Following the Glorious Revolution of 1688-1689, when Parliament had removed one king and substituted another, John Locke, an Englishman, attempted to justify this action. In his *Civil Government*, published in 1690, he stated that when a government fails to protect the natural rights of its citizens—the rights of life, liberty, and property, it surrendered its authority and could be discharged even by force if necessary.

Locke also argued that any government, in order to function effectively, needed to have three branches: the executive, the legislative, and the judicial, and that government worked best when these three branches were separate (this was the doctrine of *"separation of powers"*). Of the three, Locke considered the legislative to be the greatest (here, of course, he was arguing for the supremacy of Parliament over the king). In talking of revolution to overturn an unjust government, Locke held that people usually were slow to act; it took not merely one or two but a long series of abuses to lead them to revolution.

Locke's theory was followed in short order by that of the Frenchman Jean Jacques Rousseau, who in 1762 published his *Social Contract*. Rousseau recognized that the state had great power over its individual citizens—to command him, coerce him, even to determine what type of life he could live—but this French philosopher contended that the citizen also had rights, for government is based on a contract. Once the government is formed, the sovereign state is limited in its ability to make laws to those that bring about the general good. To administer these laws, the government has an executive branch which should be the servant of the legislative body. His emphasis in the treatise was on liberty, equality, and the supremacy of the citizen.

Thomas Jefferson had read these documents carefully, along with the works of other great thinkers of the day: Montesquieu, Hobbes, Swift, Beccaria. He knew their concepts about natural law, natural rights, and the character of British liberty. Indeed he knew of these men and their ideas, for he would write in the Declaration of Independence about "the Laws of Nature and of Nature's God." But he also was aware of the century and a half of colonial experience of Englishmen in the New World—where, in large measure, the theories about government had been put into practice even before the great men of the Age of Enlightenment gave them voice. Voltaire, a French philosopher and novelist, had written that his only regret, as part of the intellectual ferment of his age, was that he would not live to enjoy the fruits of the seed he was helping to plant. Several generations of Frenchmen would live and die before Europeans came to enjoy the freedoms about which Voltaire spoke—but in the English colonies along the Atlantic Seaboard many of those benefits had been secured to the people more than a century before—thanks to the miracle of the wilderness.

Those European philosophers and men of letters, sitting in their drawing rooms, had speculated about what men were like in a state of Nature, hoping to discover the conditions under which men lived before governments were instituted. They believed that if there were laws of Nature governing the lives of men, then the natural setting had to be recreated before these could be discerned. In the minds of these philosophers there gradually emerged a belief that these natural laws were: that the conditions of birth were identical to all men, that the life given them by Nature was an inherent right not to be taken by capricious rulers, and that the worldly goods men acquired through honest toil should be inviolable.

These were the identical rights which Englishmen had begun to realize following the winning of the Magna Carta and which had increased with each succeeding generation— until James I became king in 1603. There followed during the seventeenth century a time of turmoil and revolution, ending in 1689 with the Glorious Revolution when those rights were attained once again—only to be eroded during the eighteenth century as despotic monarchs sought to regain lost powers. Little did the English colonist realize when he left the oppression—and security—of his homeland that his desire for denied rights and the idealism of the Enlightenment would combine in the New World to allow him to live a miracle. Irony of ironies, he was moving to a continent that would allow him to return to a state of Nature where he could put into practice the visionary schemes of the new order.

The Puritan colonists who moved to Plymouth and Massachusetts Bay in 1620 and 1630 had wanted to escape a corrupt government which had refused them the right to worship in their own manner. The Mayflower Compact was an instrument of government which pledged the settlers at Plymouth to form a body politic and to submit to the will of the majority. As their villages emerged, local government was conducted through town meetings, a form of pure democracy. When Congregationalists moved west to establish a new colony, they drafted the Fundamental Orders of Connecticut; this, in effect, was a modern constitution establishing a democratic government of the "substantial" citizens.

Among these Puritans, who had come to America in part to escape religious persecution, were dissenters such as Ann Hutchinson and Roger Williams. When they experienced religious intolerance, they moved to Rhode Island, a colony of strongly individualistic and stubbornly independent people. Religious freedom also became fixed in the laws of Maryland and Pennsylvania, and the idea gradually spread.

The British king and Parliament were aware of the democratic trend in America—even encouraging it, by laws requiring the governors of the colonies to reside therein. But this was the age of mercantilism, an economic concept that argued the value of colonies for purposes of trade, therefore the British made no effort to suppress democratic tendencies, either in politics or trade. Americans later would refer to this as an age of *salutary neglect,* a time in which the colonists were allowed to develop their concepts of economics and government, when they were able to devise a system offering protection of life, liberty, and property.

John Locke

Thus by the time John Locke wrote his great essay on government, he had before him and had studied the various experiences in the English colonies. The Mayflower Compact was seventy years old, the Fundamental Orders of Connecticut almost fifty years old. When Montesquieu was writing these examples of democracy in action were yet older. Total town meetings—absolute democracy—had been in practice for more than a century when Rousseau was writing about total participatory democracy. Thomas Jefferson, Richard Henry Lee, and the other colonial political philosophers not only had the classical experiences of Greece and Rome and the writings of European thinkers but also more than a century of colonial experience fashioned by salutary neglect on which to draw. Only in America could a people transfer sovereignty from the crown to a democratic government without a traumatic break, for already they had practiced democracy for 150 years.

Thomas Jefferson, the man designated to write the Declaration of Independence, therefore was not drafting something peculiarly American, for the antecedents of what he was writing were not men but ideas. The concept of a government *"of the people, by the people, for the people"* had started in ancient Greece, had been refined in Rome, and then had begun to burst into flower in Europe during the Renaissance. Jefferson's pen would pay homage not to this man or that man but rather to the inalienable birthright of every person to a government that would protect him in his life, liberty and property.

Portrait of "His Most Sacred Majesty George III, King of Great Britain, &c.," in 1762

An Expression of the American Mind

Just as Thomas Jefferson was familiar and comfortable with the long history of man's search for a government which would guarantee his rights under the law, he knew what had caused the immediate quarrel with England. The American colonies had existed comfortably for more than a century and a half as part of the British Empire, although from the founding of the first colony the settlers in the New World had quarreled with English officials for power and control of their own destiny. Until 1763 this quarrel had always been secondary to the need for defense from French and Spanish encroachment onto lands claimed by England. The colonists, aided by British soldiers, had fought Spain and France repeatedly for mastery over the eastern part of the North American continent. Then in 1763, with the end of the Seven Years' War (or, as it was known in America, the French and Indian Wars), that threat was removed. With the needs of imperial defense satisfied, the relationship between the colonies and England naturally would change in some direction.

Aggravating the situation, however, was the British debt at the end of the Seven Years' War. The royal treasury was sadly depleted, taxes were astronomically high in England, and the debt had mounted. Because this war had been fought in large measure to protect the American colonies, members of Parliament naturally thought the Americans should contribute money both to reduce the debt and to support the British army. In short, these members were ready to end the period of salutary neglect by collecting taxes in North

Frederick North,
British Prime Minister

George Grenville,
British Prime Minister

America. Yet in doing so in the next decade, the ministers of the British government violated the Americans' concept of natural rights, especially those natural rights expressed in English statutory law. For example, the quartering of soldiers in civilian homes had ended in England prior to the time of John Locke; yet a quartering act, to be effective in the colonies, would be passed by Parliament. In short, Parliament would place greater restrictions on the colonists than were in effect in England—and the colonists naturally reacted negatively. A century and a half of freedom, of neglect, thereby would be lost. Such was the basis of the quarrel that developed between 1763 and 1776.

The quarrel began in April of 1764 when Prime Minister George Grenville by an act of Parliament imposed a tax on the colonies, known as the Sugar Act. This reduced the tax per gallon on molasses from six pence to three pence, but levied additional duties on sugar and many luxury items such as wine, coffee, silk, and linen. The act clearly implied a British determination to collect this sum, for a vice-admiralty court was created at Halifax and given jurisdiction in cases involving smuggling; previously, sympathetic juries in the colonies had freed smugglers. Moreover, the act stipulated that customs officers could not be sued for false arrest, and to aid them in their hunt for violators they were authorized to use writs of assistance (general search warrants). Finally the Sugar Act stated that all customs officers of the crown had to take up their posts in North America, not remain in England and collect their salaries as many had done previously. Grenville and his ministers hoped through the Sugar Act to raise £45,000 of the £300,000 annual cost of maintaining the royal troops in the New World.

Two additional measures, passed by the Grenville ministry in 1765, caused an even more violent reaction in the colonies: the Quartering Act and the Stamp Act. The first of these required local civil authorities to provide quarters and supplies for British troops at local expense when military barracks proved inadequate; also, part of the cost of transporting these troops within a colony had to be paid locally. The Stamp Act called for a tax in the form of stamps, costing from a halfpenny to twenty shillings, to be affixed to

Samuel Adams

Patrick Henry

all newspapers, broadsides, pamphlets, licenses, commercial bills, advertisements, almanacs, leases, playing cards, dice, and legal documents. The act did clearly state that all revenue thereby raised would be spent in the colonies, but offenses against it likewise were to be tried in the admiralty courts, not by civil juries. This measure was designed to raise an additional £60,000 annually in the colonies.

News of the passage of the Stamp Act had caused an immediate and violent reaction in America, for by no stretch of the imagination could it be termed a means of regulating trade (which even the colonists agreed Parliament had the power to do). Rather its sole and obvious purpose was to raise revenue—and it hit the most articulate classes; merchants, lawyers, clergymen, and newspapermen. The reaction took the form of constitutional opposition. In July of 1764 James Otis of Boston had issued his *Rights of the British Colonies*, a pamphlet in which he argued that there could be no taxation of the colonists without their representation in Parliament. Others, such as Daniel Dulaney of Maryland, urged the same thought, while Patrick Henry of Virginia introduced a bill in the House of Burgesses in his home colony denying the British right to tax and suggesting that George III might suffer the same fate as Julius Caesar.

On a more practical level, radical colonists took direct action by forming "Sons of Liberty" groups in Boston, New York, and other major cities to oppose enforcement of the stamp act. The Sons quickly made their presence felt through such actions as destroying the home of stamp agent Andrew Oliver in Boston, burning the records of the admiralty court there, and ransacking the home of Chief Justice Thomas Hutchinson. Soon the British revenue agents in every colony were so intimidated that many resigned their positions. Less radical than the Sons of Liberty, but equally adamant in their opposition, were members of the Stamp Act Congress, which was held in New York City during the period of October 7-25, 1765. Representatives from nine colonies gathered at the suggestion of the Massachusetts legislature to consider the "menace" to the colonies. John Dickinson's *Declaration of Rights and Grievances* was passed by this Congress; this declaration conceded that Americans owed allegiance to the British

crown, but claimed for Americans the rights of Englishmen—
including freedom from taxation without their *"own consent,
given personally, or by their representatives."* It concluded with an
appeal for repeal of the Stamp Act.

More to the point than the violence of the Sons of
Liberty or the lofty declarations of the Stamp Act Congress
were the agreements signed by merchants throughout the
colonies not to purchase any British goods. Private citizens
also agreed with this principle, stating their willingness not to
consume any British products. The non-importation, non-
consumption agreements brought business in the colonies to
a virtual standstill—and hit British merchants in their
pocketbooks. Thus the Stamp Act, when it became effective
on November 1, brought not a shower of revenue into the
royal treasury but a howl of protest from British merchants.
On December 6 some of them presented a petition to
Parliament demanding the repeal of the Stamp Act.

By this time the Grenville ministry had fallen, replaced
by the Marquis of Rockingham and his cabinet, who had to
contend with American opposition and the howls of British
merchants. In January 1766 William Pitt rose in Parliament to
demand that the Stamp Act *"be repealed absolutely, totally, and
immediately."* Pitt, the great ex-prime minister who had guided
Britain to victory in the Seven Years' War, could not be
ignored, and the Rockingham ministry gave in. On March 18
the act was repealed. However, the members of Parliament
did not want to make it appear that they had surrendered to
the colonists, therefore at the same time the Stamp Act was
repealed the Declaratory Act was passed; stating that
.Parliament and the crown had the authority to make *"laws"*
binding on the colonies *"in all cases whatsoever."* Americans were
too busy rejoicing at their victory to notice this ominous
note—which deliberately had avoided the use of the word
"tax."

Yet the British need to raise revenue was still as pressing
as it had been three years before. New monies had to be
found to support the soldiers stationed in the New World;
somehow the colonial legislatures had to be persuaded to vote
the necessary funds. Such was not to be the case, however.
On August 10, 1766, for example, the New York assembly

refused to appropriate funds for the British troops in the colony, and the next day in New York City there was a clash between the Sons of Liberty and the red-coated soldiers. Parliament responded the following year by suspending the legislative powers in the colony. At this point the British government needed a deft hand to accomplish two things: mollify the colonists yet raise money. In July of 1766 the adroit William Pitt again assumed the prime ministry. However, he became ill very soon, and control of Parliament passed to Charles Townshend, an aggressive man of superficial brilliance. Pitt might have avoided bloodshed and revolution; Townshend lacked the ability to avoid conflict.

Serving as minister of the Exchequer in the ministry of the Duke of Grafton, Townshend came to office determined to raise money in the colonies. He hoped to do this under the guise of regulating commerce, something which the colonists had always conceded Parliament had the right to do.

On July 2, 1767, the Townshend Revenue Act and the Customs Collecting Act were passed. The latter created four new vice-admiralty courts in the colonies and revised the methods of enforcing the revenue acts. The Townshend duties, as they came to be known, consisted of taxes on lead, paint, glass, and tea. These were low—but they were attached to articles of common use and tended to raise the cost of living generally.

The £40,000 which would be raised by the Townshend duties was to be used to pay the salaries of colonial judges and other officials, who previously had been dependent on colonial legislatures for their funds. Thus these officials were to be freed from this restraint. Moreover, the Townshend duties provided that writs of assistance (blank search warrants) could be used; and admiralty courts, not civil juries, were to try offenders.

Resistance to the Townshend duties was quickly forthcoming. On October 28 in Boston a non-importation, non-consumption agreement was drafted by merchants, an idea that quickly spread to other colonies. As a result imports from England dropped drastically—from £1,363,000 in 1768 to £504,000 in 1769. This had the desired effect on British merchants who quickly made known their anger to members of Parliament. On a more philosophical level, John Dickinson published his protest in his *Letters of a Pennsylvania Farmer* between December 1767 and February 1768; a Philadelphia lawyer, Dickinson conceded that Parliament had the authority to regulate trade—but not for the purpose of raising revenue. Therefore he concluded that the Townshend duties violated the unwritten British constitution, for the taxes amounted to taxation without representation. Moreover, he asserted that Parliament's suspension of the New York legislature was a threat to the liberties of all the colonies; what could be done in one colony could be done in any of the others.

On February 11, 1768, Samuel Adams drafted the Massachusetts Circular Letter. In this Adams restated the arguments of Dickinson and urged united colonial action to resist unconstitutional taxation; moreover, he said that Americans could never be represented in Parliament, for this was impractical, and he opposed any British efforts to pay colonial officials' salaries from the royal treasury. This letter was sent to the other colonial legislatures as a statement of the feelings in Massachusetts, so angering the royal governor there that he dissolved the legislature of the colony. Customs agents in Boston asked for military support in collecting the taxes, and two regiments under General Thomas Gage arrived in Boston in September for that purpose.

Adams' letter had the desired effect of stirring the other colonies. In Virginia, for example, George Washington introduced the *Virginia Resolves* in the House of Burgesses. These resolutions stated that the colonies could be taxed only by their own legislative bodies, not by Parliament. The governor of Virginia responded to the Resolves by dissolving the House of Burgesses, while in England the House of Lords recommended that the colonial rebels be tried for treason. By January of 1770, insurrection was a definite threat. A strong king might have avoided war at this point, but George III was ill prepared to be conciliatory or to make compromises.

Born in 1738, George III was the third Hanoverian King to come to the throne of England. His great-grandfather, George I, a great-grandson of James I, had inherited the English throne in 1714 upon the death of Queen Anne, who was without children. A native of the German province of

Hanover, and unable to speak English, George I allowed his ministers to run the country. He was succeeded upon his death in 1727 by his son. Also a native of Hanover, George II had little ambition (or culture) and thus left most matters of state to his ministers.

George III, born in England, was educated by the Earl of Harcourt and the Bishop of Norwich, men who taught him to believe in the divine right of kings and the necessity of ruling absolutely. Upon the death of George II in 1760, he assumed the throne determined to reduce the power of Parliament. During the first years of his reign, he learned that he needed a pliant prime minister and strong backing to accomplish his goals. Thus he formed what amounted to his own political party, the king's friends, and Frederick Lord North became prime minister. For twelve years George III, through Lord North, would rule England.

Acting on the king's orders, Lord North heeded the plea of British merchants—as well as common sense, which dictated that the Townshend duties were bringing in less money than they were costing—and asked Parliament to repeal these taxes, at least, all of them except the one on tea. This one was kept as a matter of principle, an assertion of the king's power to tax the colonies. This measure passed on April 12, while the Quartering Act was allowed to expire. Peace seemed about to return. But while Parliament was debating repeal of the Townshend duties, blood was being shed in Boston.

On March 5 British soldiers in the Massachusetts city were harassed by a mob. In panic the soldiers fired into the crowd, killing five and wounding six. The troops' defense was recognized as legal, and they were defended at their trial by John Adams and Josiah Quincy, both prominent leaders of the Patriot group. The soldiers were acquitted of murder, but among the Sons of Liberty the incident was popularized as "the Boston Massacre."

The year 1771 was one of comparative peace. Colonial merchants had turned conservative as a result of their rising fear that acts of violence by the Sons of Liberty would get out of hand. Riots such as the Boston Massacre had appalled the merchants. Samuel Adams and his like-minded fellow Patriots

The Boston Massacre, March 5, 1770

(engraving by Paul Revere)

tried to keep alive the spirit of resistance by creating
Committees of Correspondence, which Adams formed in
Boston in 1772. The idea spread to other colonies, and they
wrote to each other to report British outrages. One incident
which the Patriots wrote about was the burning of the *Gaspee*,
a British revenue cutter which ran aground in Rhode Island
on June 9, 1772, at Narragansett Bay; Rhode Islanders
swarmed aboard and set it afire, and no witnesses could be
found to identify the culprits.

The course toward revolution yet might have been
changed by men of good will on both sides. Such was not to
be the case, however. The Americans had begun to believe
their arguments that they could not be taxed without
representation in Parliament, for such was the traditional
right of Englishmen. To rejoinders that they were "virtually"
represented in Parliament—which was an English argument
that held that all Englishmen were represented in
Parliament—the colonists replied that while this might satisfy
legal arguments in England it did nothing for them; in short,
they were arguing that they were united to England only by
loyalty to the crown and that only their own legislatures
could tax them. They had evolved what would be called the
Commonwealth or Dominion concept at a latter date, and
they saw themselves as conservators of traditional British
liberties and freedoms at a time when these freedoms were
gradually being lost in England to a king determined to rule in
the old style. In England itself, the colonial arguments carried
little weight. Both the Tory and Whig parties asserted the
right of Parliament to legislate for the colonies in every way,
including taxation, and they believed in the right of the crown
to veto any colonial law.

The crux of the matter, therefore, was taxation without
representation. The Americans opposed British-imposed
taxes, while the English government was opposed to
representative government in the colonies. Meanwhile,
neither the Tories, who supported George III, nor the Whigs,
who opposed the king, were willing to allow the colonists to
elect men to represent them in Parliament.

This argument came to a head over the Tea Act, which
was passed on May 10, 1773, to save the East India Company

from bankruptcy. This company, whose stockholders were influential in British politics, had no money but 17,000,000 pounds of tea; it was granted the right to sell this tea directly to the colonies without first bringing it to England (as other merchants had to do), and it was to get a share of all taxes paid on the commodity in the colonies. Merchants in New York and Philadelphia protested that the tax on tea should not be paid, although it was far less than Englishmen themselves were paying on tea. The Massachusetts Committee of Correspondence advised that all East India Company tea should not be allowed to land in the New World. On December 16, after a town meeting in Boston at which Samuel Adams declared, *This meeting can do nothing more to save the country,* a group of "Patriots" disguised themselves as Indians and boarded three ships in the harbor to dump the tea into the sea. The Boston Tea Party brought to a head the question of home rule, it committed the patriots to violent action, it inflamed British public opinion against Americans, and it strengthened the hand of the conservatives in Parliament who were supporting George III. The Boston Tea Party thus set colonials and Englishmen on a collision course that could be resolved only with sword and musket.

The king, the North ministry, Parliament—the whole structure of British control over the colonies—could not disregard the Boston Tea Party. On March 4, 1774, Parliament was summoned into session to punish Massachusetts for the defiance of its citizens. Between March 31 and June 2, four measures were passed into law. The first of these, the Boston Port Bill, closed Boston harbor and moved the capital of the colony, along with the customs office, to Salem; no ships could call at Boston after June 1 until the East India Company and the customs officers had been paid for their losses, estimated at £15,000. The Massachusetts Government Act came next. This lessened democratic government in the colony by providing that the upper chamber of the legislature thereafter would be appointed, not elected as previously; the governor would appoint lesser judges and nominate for royal appointment the superior judges; juries would be chosen by the sheriff rather than by election; and town meetings could not be called without the consent of the governor.

The third measure, called the Administration of Justice Act, stated that anyone charged with a capital offense would be tried in England if the governor thought the accused could not get a fair trial in the colony. Finally, the Quartering Act of 1765 was revived, and the royal governor was replaced by General Thomas Gage, who became the colony's chief executive.

These four measures, known in England as the Coercive Acts, promptly were dubbed the Intolerable Acts in America. Samuel Adams through his Committee of Correspondence was quick to remind residents of other colonies that what could happen in Massachusetts could just as readily happen elsewhere. Then, as word of the Intolerable Acts was spreading, news came that Parliament had passed the Quebec Act. This measure, which Parliament enacted on June 22, 1774, annexed to the province of Quebec (Canada) all territory north of the Ohio River, thereby nullifying the western land claims of four colonies and threatening the profits of many companies—and individuals—speculating in land. Further, the Quebec Act stipulated that all furs gathered in the interior of North America be shipped from Montreal rather than from New Orleans or any other port, and it recognized Catholicism as an approved religion by allowing Catholics to sit in the assembly of Quebec. Finally, it provided that Canadians could use French civil law rather than English common law in their trials. The passage of the Quebec Act caused widespread opposition in the colonies— and even more widespread fear. New Englanders resented the benefits granted to Catholics, which they believed to be contrary to English law. And the use of French civil law meant trials without jury, a practice abhorrent to Englishmen. Finally, the loss of the western lands in the Ohio Valley and the channeling of the fur trade through Canada meant a loss of profits for many Americans.

The reaction to the events of the spring of 1774 came in the form of a plethora of pamphlets. Thomas Jefferson's *A Summary View of the Rights of British America* rejected the concept that Parliament was all-powerful, stating that the colonists need only obey the king. James Wilson of Pennsylvania wrote in a similar vein. Even Edmund Burke, a noted British writer

"The Bostonian's Paying the Excise-Man, or Tarring & Feathering"
(printed in London in October of 1774)

and philosopher, wrote to the New York assembly from London to say that the purpose of the Quebec Act was to halt the growth of the American colonies and to deprive the residents of the New World of their traditional British liberties. The Massachusetts House of Representatives was more direct than any philosopher, however; it sent a letter asking all the colonies to send delegates to Philadelphia to a Continental Congress, which it suggested should meet the first week in September, 1774.

On September 5 delegates from twelve colonies attended this First Continental Congress. Only Georgia was unrepresented. The stated purpose of the meeting was to *"consult upon the present unhappy state of the colonies."* The delegates had been chosen by the Committees of Correspondence and therefore consisted of such radicals as John and Samuel Adams of Massachusetts, Patrick Henry and Richard Henry Lee of Virginia, and Christopher Gadsden of South Carolina; moderates such as Peyton Randolph and George Washington of Virginia, John Jay of New York, and John Dickinson of Pennsylvania; and conservatives such as Joseph Galloway of Pennsylvania. This extra-legal body faced a dilemma; it was expected to ward off Parliamentary wrath, restore imperial relations to a happy keel, and yet assert colonial rights. The members had to put forward a firm and forceful front to gain the concessions they wanted, yet they could not leave themselves open to accusations of radicalism either from American conservatives or British friends. In short, they had to brandish the sword, and simultaneously extend the olive branch.

Two plans were advocated in this congress, one conservative and the other radical. Joseph Galloway proposed to the body a Plan of Union, which called for a separate American government consisting of a President General, appointed by the king, and a legislative council chosen by the colonial legislatures; no act of Parliament would apply in America unless approved by this body, itself to be an inferior branch of Parliament, and it would control Indian affairs in North America, western lands, and men and money in time of war. Galloway's Plan of Union was defeated probably because of false rumors that General Gage had bombarded Boston.

Instead, Congress voted to endorse the Suffolk Resolves
(taken from a convention in Suffolk County, Massachusetts);
these stated that the Intolerable Acts should be resisted *"as the
attempts of a wicked administration to enslave America,"* that the
colonies should raise troops, and that all Americans should
join in non-importation and non-exportation of goods to or
from England, Ireland, and the British West Indies.

On October 14, 1774, came a more philosophical
statement, a "Declaration of Rights and Resolves," from
Congress. This condemned the Intolerable Acts, taxation of
the colonies, and the large British army in America; it listed
the rights of the colonists, among which were "life, liberty,
and property," a phrase borrowed from John Locke; and it
asserted that England had only the power to regulate external
trade and legislate for imperial affairs. The "Declaration" in
reality was addressed to George III and to the people of
England, as much as to Parliament, and was conciliatory in
tone, although if accepted it would have limited the king's
power over the colonies.

Just before it adjourned, this Congress established a
Continental Association—a system of committees of
inspection in towns and counties in all the colonies to
supervise the non-importation, non-exportation of goods to
and from England. This Association was charged to inspect
customs entries, publish the names of violators, and to
confiscate British goods. Thus a Congress called to protest
against a Parliamentary usurpation of rights ended by
creating a powerful extra-legal machinery for the supervision
of American life. Then, just as it adjourned, the Congress
agreed that unless its demands had been met, it would
reconvene on May 10, 1775.

During that fall of 1774, public opinion in America split
into two positions: Patriot and Loyalist. Attacks on Loyalists
increased during the autumn months of 1774. Their property
was confiscated in some areas, and tar and feathers were
liberally applied to those who stated a wish to remain loyal to
England. "Minutemen" began drilling openly on village
greens, while the Continental Association published the
names of those who imported or consumed British goods;
these lists appeared in newspapers under the heading

"enemies of *American* liberty." Arms and ammunition were stored, especially in New England, as men prepared to fight for their rights as Englishmen against the usurpations of king, Parliament, or any other group. The clouds of war were darkening—and ominous with thunder.

On January 19, 1775, the petition of the Continental Congress was laid before Parliament. A majority of the members of that body supported their king, unaware that his intention of suppressing the colonies was, in reality, a threat to their own liberties and freedoms. On February 9 the members voted that Massachusetts was in a state of rebellion, although Lord North did on February 27 push through a resolution, known as the Plan of Conciliation, which stated that Parliament would tax no colony that would tax itself for the cost of its government and its share of the costs of imperial defense.

The time for conciliation had passed. On March 23 in Virginia, Patrick Henry asserted a truth so bitter as to be forgotten easily; life, he said, was not so sweet as to be bought at the price of chains and slavery. His "liberty or death" speech set the mood and tone for Americans.

The British response to the continued opposition in New England was to order General Gage on April 14 to use force to end the rebellion. Five days later Gage sent seven hundred troops to seize arms and supplies at Concord, twenty miles northwest of Boston. Patriots in Boston managed to send riders to spread the alarm, and minutemen gathered along the route of march. At Lexington Green the British troops fired at Americans, killing eight, then proceeded to Concord. Failing to find the munitions, which had been moved, the troops began a return march to Boston—which proved a long, bloody trail. Minutemen by the thousands fired on them, killing or wounding 247 of them while sustaining only 95 casualties themselves. Thus by the time the Second Continental Congress met in Philadelphia on May 10, 1775, the war was one of bullets, not words, of sword and musket, not pamphlet and petition.

At this Second Continental Congress, the membership was distinguished. Among its members were John and Samuel Adams of Massachusetts, Benjamin Franklin of

The Battle at Concord Bridge (engraved by W. J. Edwards)

Pennsylvania, John Jay of New York, and Thomas Jefferson and Richard Henry Lee of Virginia. Elected president of the Congress was John Hancock of Massachusetts. The Congress quickly moved to exercise the powers of sovereignty. It authorized an army and created a navy; it appointed George Washington commander-in-chief of the army; it established a postal system and a treasury; it issued paper money and floated loans; it negotiated treaties with Indian tribes; it sent diplomatic agents abroad to seek aid; and it tried to provide for defense of the frontier. At the same time, however, it made attempts to conciliate England. On July 5 it adopted the Olive Branch Petition, authored by John Dickinson, which was an appeal to George III to restrain Parliament from passing further tyrannical measures. The next day, however, the Congress adopted a Declaration of Causes and Necessities of Taking up Arms, written by Thomas Jefferson and John Dickinson. This statement was intended to aid the American cause in England, for it asserted, "We have not raised armies with ambitious designs of separating from Great Britain, and establishing independence." Yet at the same time it hinted that foreign assistance was available to aid the colonies, and it stated that Americans were "resolved to die free men rather than live slaves." This work done, the Congress adjourned on August 2.

George III dashed any hopes the colonists might have harbored that their grievances were all at the hands of Parliament, not the crown. His reaction to the Olive Branch Petition and the Declaration of Causes and Necessities of Taking up Arms came on August 23 when he proclaimed that Americans were rebels and warned loyal subjects to refrain from giving them assistance. Yet in his attempts to suppress the rebellion, George III found little popular support from his subjects at home. Previously in Europe, kings had been able to raise armies with some ease, for the people knew armies had to exist to preserve internal peace or to meet some external threat. Therefore when a king needed an army, he issued a call, and men everywhere in the country responded, either to fight for the king (or some would-be king) or else to protect the nation. The Americans were fighting for an idea, but in England this motivation was lacking; in fact, so few

Englishmen were willing to join the army of George III in 1775 that he and his ministers had to hire 30,000 mercenaries, usually called "Hessians" because so many of them came from the Grand Duchy of Hesse, Germany. This move, along with his other policies, helped widen the gulf between colonies and England—and drove Americans toward an open declaration of independence.

When the Continental Congress reconvened on September 12, 1775, its mood was more radical. During that winter, as the war raged, still more converts were made for the Patriot cause, and the Congress had to assume yet more of the powers of sovereignty. On April 6, 1776, for example, the Congress opened American ports to commerce from all nations except England, which in itself was virtually a declaration of independence. Then on May 10 Congress took yet another step by recommending that the thirteen colonies (and all now were represented in the Congress) should form their own governments "such as shall best conduce to the happiness and safety of their constituents." Four colonies already had taken this step by that time.

Then on June 7, 1776, Richard Henry Lee of Virginia introduced a "Resolution of Independence" in Congress. This stated *"That these United Colonies are, and of a right ought to be, free and independent States, that they are absolved of all allegiance to the British Crown...."* Four days later Congress appointed a committee of Jefferson, John Adams, Franklin, Roger Sherman, and Robert Livingston to prepare a draft of a formal resolution. Thus Thomas Jefferson came to his second-floor lodgings at Market and Seventh streets in Philadelphia to put into words the thoughts, hopes, and aspirations of his fellow countrymen.

The words that flowed from Jefferson's pen were drawn thus from the philosophical doctrines then current and from the immediate course of events prior to 1776. The document contained a brief preamble in which he stated that "When in the course of human events it becomes necessary for one people to dissolve the political bands which have connected them with another," some justification was necessary. There followed a second part of the Declaration, one giving the political theories underlying the revolution. Jefferson began that section with a statement often quoted since: "all men are created equal." Certainly in 1776 all men were not equal in colonial society. Slaves were openly owned in many parts of America, while in all the colonies only men of wealth, position, and membership in a certain church could hold office—or even vote. Yet Jefferson was asserting as a matter of principle that all men were equal, a declaration that would allow a gradual change in society in the years that followed— or, as Jefferson perhaps foresaw, a statement that would allow for a gradual broadening of the suffrage and the base of society. In the lines that followed, he included the ideas of John Locke, stating that among man's inalienable rights were "Life, Liberty and the pursuit of Happiness." For his own reasons he chose to substitute "the pursuit of Happiness" for Locke's third right, that of property. He concluded that the purpose of government was to protect these rights and that, inasmuch as governments draw "their just power from the consent of the governed," they could legitimately be overthrown when they no longer met the needs of the governed.

Section three of the Declaration was a listing of violations of the "social contract" by George III. In all he listed eighteen ways in which "the present King of Great Britain" was guilty of "repeated injuries and usurpations, all having in direct object the establishment of an absolute Tyranny over these States." The king had vetoed colonial laws, had dissolved colonial legislatures, had tried to limit the growth of the colonies, had obstructed the administration of justice, had sought to make judges answerable only to the crown, had kept a standing army in the colonies in time of peace, had quartered troops among the civil population, had imposed taxes without the consent of the people, had denied trial by jury, and had cut off external trade.

Section four of the Declaration reviewed the unsuccessful colonial attempts to secure redress from the repeated injuries: "In every stage of these Oppressions We have Petitioned for Redress in the most humble terms: Our repeated Petitions have been answered only by repeated injury." Thus, concluded Jefferson, George III had clearly marked himself a tyrant, one "unfit to be the ruler of a free

People." Jefferson continued this section by noting that the colonies had appealed to the British people directly, telling them that the king was subverting justice in the New World. However, these appeals, directed at the British people's native justice and magnanimity," had fallen on deaf ears.

The last section of the Document asserted the independence of the colonies: "That these United Colonies are, and of Right ought to be Free and Independent States; that they are Absolved from all Allegiance to the British Crown, and that all political connection between them and the State of Great Britain, is and ought to be totally dissolved." He concluded by stating that the signers of this Declaration did so "with a firm reliance on the Protection of Divine Providence" and to that end "we mutually pledge to each other our Lives, our Fortunes and our sacred Honor."

Beginning sometime after June 11 on this exercise, Jefferson concluded his labors by June 28. By that date he copied all his thoughts onto a rough draft (which has survived). This in hand, he met with Adams and Franklin to get their suggestions. Jefferson's copy of the rough draft, which has survived, shows that the two men indeed made suggestions which were incorporated into the copy that was submitted to Congress.

The members of the Continental Congress knew that a vote for this Declaration was an act of treason against the British crown—and that they were pledging their lives, fortunes, and sacred honor on a successful conclusion to the war. However, these men were representatives of the people of the individual colonies, and in each of these colonies there already had been incidents inclining the people to accept a final break with England.

"The First Prayer in Congress, September 1774 in Carpenters Hall, Philadelphia"
(early steel engraving)

The Trying of Men's Souls

John Murray, Earl of Dunmore, Viscount Fincastle, Baron of Blair and of Moulin and of Tillymount, arrived in Virginia in 1771 as royal governor. This young Scottish nobleman, not yet forty years of age, at first was immensely popular in the colony. At the governor's palace in Williamsburg he entertained the colonial gentry, while his newborn daughter, whom he named Virginia, was adopted by the colony. However, Lord Dunmore was a haughty aristocrat, one who for nine years had served in Parliament as a peer from Scotland. Living in London, he had dined often with statesmen and nobility, and thus he distrusted the rude colonials among whom he lived.

In 1773 came the first open break between the governor and his constituents. When the call came for committees of correspondence and the House of Burgesses concurred, Dunmore dissolved this legislative body, writing tartly to a friend in England, "There are some resolves which show a little ill humor in the House of Burgesses. . . ." Then in May 1774 the legislature again was called into session—just in time to hear of the Boston Port Act. Virginians knew the enforcement of this act would ruin the prosperous commercial city of Boston, and they realized that what could be done to Massachusetts could also be done to their colony. Therefore Thomas Jefferson and other members of the House of Burgesses introduced a bill calling for a day of fasting and prayer in the colony for "our sister colony of Massachusetts Bay." Dunmore, feeling that this measure reflected badly on the king and Parliament, dissolved the House a second time.

Despite these actions, there was no widespread feeling in Virginia that Americans should seek their independence from England. Not until late in 1775 would such thoughts surface—and then with growing force. By that time, when the Second Continental Congress was sitting and shots had been fired in Massachusetts, Lord Dunmore decided to remove all available gunpowder to a British man-of-war, the *Fowey*, and thereafter he would conduct his business from that safe retreat. Members of the House of Burgesses, called to meet that summer, pressed the governor to pay for the gunpowder which he had moved. By November the governor was so embittered that he declared martial law in the colony and suggested that the slaves in it should revolt against their masters. Both these moves further alienated even conservative Virginians and led to yet more talk of independence. Then on December 9 that same year, behind British troops, Lord Dunmore came ashore. Meeting stout resistance, he fought the Battle of Great Bridge. Soundly defeated, he and his troops returned to the ships, from which on January 1, 1776, he directed the bombardment of Norfolk, which burned. (Jefferson, in the Declaration of Independence, made reference to this act when he commented that the king was responsible for those who had "ravaged our coasts, burnt our towns, and destroyed the lives of our people.")

Actions such as those of Lord Dunmore, repeated in other colonies on a lesser scale, were responsible for convincing a growing number of Americans that they should think of separation from England. Yet what had begun largely as a struggle to retain the traditional rights of Englishmen— as Americans saw these—did not change overnight to demand for independence. Rather that movement was slow. When the Second Continental Congress convened on May 10, 1775, for example, the members specifically disavowed any intent of separation; in its Declaration of the Causes and Necessity of Taking Up Arms, passed on July 6, 1775, the members reaffirmed their membership in the British Empire. These men thought of themselves as loyal subjects of the British crown. George III might yet have avoided the loss of the colonies had he been willing to retreat from his demands for absolute sovereignty; instead he aided the radical cause in

America when he rejected the Olive Branch Petition and proclaimed the colonies in open rebellion. When Congress reconvened that fall, the members rejected the king's statement but still—even then—acknowledged the sovereignty of George III.

Lord Dunmore's actions on January 1, 1776, in firing the city of Norfolk and his previous call on the slaves to revolt—and news of both these events were widely circulated by the radicals—widened the rift between colonies and mother country, just as did the British hiring of mercenaries to fight in America. As word spread that thousands of Hessians were on their way to the colonies, the American mood shifted increasingly to thoughts of independence from so callous a nation as England.

Then in January of 1776 came the publication of a pamphlet entitled *Common Sense*, the work of a thirty-nine-year-old former British corsetmaker and civil servant who had been in the New World just one year. Thomas Paine, the author of this remarkable document, had been born in 1737 in Thetford, England. He had attended grammar school until age thirteen when he was apprenticed as a corsetmaker, a task he followed for six years until he left home to fight at sea as a privateer. In the years that followed he was employed in a variety of occupations: schoolteacher, exciseman, tobacconist, grocer, and, of course, corsetmaker. All the while he was secretly angry at his poverty and his inability to advance himself materially, but at the same time he read voraciously, thought long, and gradually formulated revolutionary doctrines within his heart.

Arriving at Philadelphia late in 1774, he became a journalist, supporting himself by writing for the *Pennsylvania Magazine* on a diversity of subjects including the abolition of slavery. Aware of the currents of war sweeping the country, Paine in January of 1776 drafted his thoughts on the war with England and published these in a forty-seven-page pamphlet which sold for a modest two shillings. As was the custom of the day, he published his effort anonymously. In the drafting of this work, which sold an astonishing 120,000 copies in just three months, Paine had consulted Dr. Benjamin Rush of Philadelphia, a leading scientist of the day,

Thomas Paine

and possibly Benjamin Franklin. Because the journalistic style was so clear and brisk, many readers attributed the work to Franklin, but in its revolutionary fervor *Common Sense* was clearly the work of a man who loved freedom.

Paine was one of the first to see a divine mission for America; "The sun never shined on a cause more just," he wrote, for the cause of America was that of mankind itself. If America would but free itself of the tyranny of monarchy, declared Paine, it would set an example for all the world and thereby would alter the destiny of man.

A declaration of independence, he argued, was "common sense" because the colonies did not need England for reasons of defense; France and Spain, who had been the enemy in so many previous wars, did not hate Americans but rather the British; if America separated from England, it would not have these two nations as opponents. Furthermore, he said it was absurd for an island to govern a continent—which he equated with the tail wagging the dog; and he insisted that American goods would insure prosperity without English connections; Europeans had to eat and thus would buy America's produce. Finally, he argued that if it was wrong for America to break away from England, then that same argument meant that England still should be governed by France. In sum, wrote Paine, independence was both logical and necessary.

Thomas Paine's call for independence echoed the work of the radicals who were using the committees of correspondence to good effect. Later such work would be called "psychological warfare"; in 1776, however, this meant only a constant writing of letters calling for vigorous opposition to George III and the usurpations of Parliament. And that same month of January 1776, General George Washington publicly declared himself in favor of independence, a statement that carried great public weight because of Washington's stature.

Congress on April 6 responded to the growing popular support for independence—and the fighting which was raging—by opening American ports to commerce from all nations except England. Early in May John Adams of Massachusetts brought yet another step along the road to independence when he introduced a resolution in Congress,

Richard Henry Lee

Joseph Galloway

one which urged each of the colonies to form their own
governments "such as shall best conduce to the happiness and
safety of their constituents." The preamble to this resolution
stated that each colony should exercise complete control over
its own affairs and, in the process, suppress all royal
authority. Delegates of the middle colonies hesitated to take
this step, for it amounted to a declaration of independence.
However, the delegates from New England and the Southern
colonies (Virginia, the Carolinas, and Georgia) had no such
hesitation, and after five days of debate the measure passed.
Actually four colonies already had established such local
government, and by 1777 all except Massachusetts,
Connecticut, and Rhode Island had written new constitutions.
Adams saw his resolution of May 10 as "the most important
Resolution that ever was taken in America," but it merely
was a preliminary to the formal declaration that followed
shortly.

The final push for a declaration of independence came
because of a torrent of letters arriving in Philadelphia from
constituents of the members of the Continental Congress. In
North Carolina, a colony of independent-minded citizens
where separatist sentiment was high, the Provincial Congress
(legislature) on April 12 passed a resolution calling on the
delegates of that colony to support a bill of "Independency" in
the Continental Congress. The following month the House of
Burgesses in Virginia likewise passed such a bill, this one
instructing the Virginia delegates to press Congress to pass
such a measure. Coupled with these instructions was a
reference to the necessity of independence to secure foreign
aid in the fight against Great Britain, and the Virginia
resolution spoke of the need for colonial confederation.

The resolution from Virginia, along with the one from
North Carolina, was presented in Congress on May 27, but
both lay on the table for ten days while other issues were
debated. Then on June 7 Richard Henry Lee of Virginia
introduced a "Resolution of Independence" in which he
pressed three matters: (1) "That these United Colonies are,
and of right ought to be, free and independent States, that
they are absolved from all allegiance to the British
Crown... " (2) "That it is expedient forthwith to take the

most effectual measures for forming foreign Alliances." And
(3) "That a plan of confederation be prepared and transmitted
to the respective Colonies for their consideration and
approbation."

John Adams hurried to second this proposal—the
delegates from Virginia and Massachusetts already had found
themselves thinking and acting in accord on many measures.
In the debate which followed Adams and Lee worked to gain
support for the resolution, to be joined by George Wythe, the
great legal authority from Williamsburg. Yet there was
opposition from delegates from South Carolina, New York,
and Pennsylvania, so the debate was postponed until these
delegates might ascertain the wishes of their constituents, for
all members of Congress realized the need of presenting a
united front on so important an issue. Yet because all realized
that a declaration was almost inevitable, Congress on June 11
appointed a committee to prepare a draft copy of a formal
resolution of independence. The document was ready on June
28, at which time the committee presented it to Congress. It
lay on the table until the delegates had decided on Lee's
original resolution.

On July 1 debate on this resolution resumed. At this time
Congress resolved itself into a committee of the whole to
debate the measure. John Hancock gave up his chair as
presiding officer to join the debate; filling the chair was portly
Benjamin Harrison of Virginia. In the voting that followed,
each state, no matter how large its delegation, had one vote.
Nine of the thirteen states immediately voted for Lee's
resolution. The delegates from New York were expecting to
hear from their legislature and abstained until that word
arrived; the two delegates from Delaware split their vote and
thus could not yet be tallied; and the delegates from
Pennsylvania and South Carolina voted negatively.

John Dickinson of Pennsylvania appeared to be the
leading spokesman against the resolution, but his argument
was not in opposition to independence so much as against the
timing of the measure. Because a new slate of delegates had
arrived from New Jersey and stated that they wished to hear
both sides of the case, John Adams rose to speak in behalf of
the resolution. He protested that he had made no special

preparation and that he was a poor speaker, yet his words carried weight for he was widely known for his fiery patriotism to the American cause. Born in 1735, he had considered becoming a minister while a youth, but "frigid John Calvin" and "disputed points" of doctrine had changed his mind. Instead he graduated from Harvard to become a lawyer and a leader in Massachusetts. Married to Abigail Smith in 1764, he was a man of great strength and vigor—and a highly developed sense of right; he pushed the colonial cause because he thought that acts of the British Parliament and king were wrong, yet he also defended the conduct of the British soldiers involved in the so-called Boston Massacre in 1770 because he thought they had acted in legal fashion.

At the time Adams spoke to the Continental Congress in favor of the Declaration of Independence, he was, according to Jefferson's account, "not graceful nor eloquent, nor remarkably fluent, but he came out occasionally with a power of thought and expression that moved us from our seats." Apparently his words did sway the delegates from New Jersey, for they indicated a willingness to vote for the measure. The South Carolinians the following day decided to change their vote. Thus at the end of the first day, the committee of the whole asked leave to sit again the following day.

On July 2, with eleven colonies in favor of the resolution, the delegates from Pennsylvania acceded; in fact, two opponents of independence deliberately stayed away, allowing a majority of the remaining delegates to vote in favor of the measure. This left only Delaware in opposition—and a dramatic ride by an absent delegate swung the vote of that colony. Patriots in Congress who favored independence had sent a hasty summons to Caesar Rodney, one of the missing delegates from Delaware, one who favored breaking with England, and he rode eighty miles—night and day through a rain storm—to arrive in time to break the tie in his delegation's vote and thus swing Delaware into the column favoring the measure. This made the vote of the committee of the whole unanimous except for New York, which would abstain until July 15 (six days previously the legislature of that colony voted for independence, and when word of this

Congress voting independence
(engraving by Edward Savage, after Robert Edge Pine and Edward Savage)

action reached Philadelphia the delegates from New York added their assent, making the final vote unanimous).

This vote on July 2 assured a declaration of independence. Thus when the delegates again went into regular session, rather than as a committee of the whole, the discussion was about the substance of the declaration, not about independence itself. (John Adams in later years would argue that July 2 should be the date when Americans celebrated independence, not July 4.) When the delegates began debating the form of the declaration, they had Jefferson's document ready before them.

This "rough draft" which came from Jefferson's pen was not considered sacrosanct by the delegates. In fact, they made more than eighty changes in the original. Most of these were mere word changes; for example, where Jefferson had written "We hold these truths to be sacred and undeniable," Congress substituted that these truths were "Self-evident." In the discussion on the floor, which occurred on July 3 and 4, Jefferson sat silent—as behooved the author; however, he must have fumed inwardly, for later he commented about the "depredations" which his handiwork suffered during those two days. John Adams spoke strongly in favor of the document, and in the end even the Congressmen, who struck out several of Jefferson's more lilting phrases, left in his final passage to the effect that "we mutually pledge to each other our Lives, our Fortunes, and our sacred Honor." The end result was a masterpiece even more tightly written than it had come from Jefferson's pen, one that became even more than a political statement; rather it was a hymn about the eternal independence of the human spirit, a piece of lyric poetry that would inspire men from July 4, 1776, to the present. Certainly it was a document which embodied the aspirations of the patriots of the colonies.

The gentlemen in Philadelphia who voted for this declaration may not have realized fully the great significance of their words. When they declared that *all men are created equal,*" their words came from the heat of their quarrel with England. No doubt, they had not thought this idea through to its logical conclusion, for some of them owned slaves at the time. This statement would place them and their descendants

in jeopardy from those segments of the population which in
1776 did not have equality; those words planted the seeds of a
continuing American revolution, one that has continued for
two centuries and which shows no sign of slowing. Yet
Jefferson in drafting these words and the delegates in voting
for them had caught the true spirit of America, for it has
been an American characteristic to make an idealistic
statement, then compromise it in the name of pragmatism,
and then begin to feel guilty that the country has not lived up
to its own expectations. The continuing revolution has its
origins there, for the nation gradually has tried to match its
pragmatism to its idealism. The Declaration of Independence
was not racial; it was not white or black or red or yellow.
Rather it was a statement of an idea and an ideal toward
which America could work.

The vote on the document taken on July 4, it was signed
by President John Hancock and Secretary Charles Thomson.
That evening, at the instructions of Congress, the original
committee of five took the copy to printer John Dunlap. Some
students of the document have asserted that Dunlap inserted
punctuation and capital letters to fit his own whims about
grammar—but the resulting broadside publication certainly
was a pleasing piece of typography. The following day, July 5,
the official copy was inserted into a blank page left for the
purpose in the rough Journal of Congress, and this became
the official copy. Eventually fifty-five of the delegates would
sign it. Other broadside copies, printed by Dunlap, were sent
to the legislatures of all the "states" and to the army.

When the declaration was read to an assemblage of
people in Philadelphia, one observer wrote that the crowd
contained "few respectable people." In truth this declaration
created real problems for those still loyal to England—and
many of the prosperous residents of Philadelphia still believed
themselves to be Englishmen. After the Declaration of
Independence was proclaimed, however, the United States
was committed to a total war with England, and the Loyalists
had to take a stand—for loyalty to the king had become
treason to the young nation. In most colonies the Patriots
organized committees to force everyone to take an oath of
allegiance to the United States on pain of imprisonment of

person and confiscation of property for failure to do so. The
Loyalists—some estimates of their number run as high as
one-third of all the people in the United States—were
impressive both in numbers and in quality. In some of the
states, such as New York, New Jersey, and Georgia, they
possibly were in the majority. Royal officials, Anglican clergy,
and great landowners (except in Virginia) tended toward
loyalty, while merchants were about evenly divided. Most
Loyalists took the Patriot oath and paid their taxes while
secretly praying for the defeat of Washington's army; others
fled behind British lines or to Florida, Canada, or England.
Some enlisted and fought on the British side; there were
several Tory companies in the Southern states, while an
estimated 15,000 New Yorkers became British troops.

The course of the war was strange. Americans tended to
lose the battles, but in the end they triumphed. Leading them
in this fight was George Washington. Appointed commander-
in-chief on June 15 by the Continental Congress, Washington
was more than just a man; he was a symbol, an embodiment
of the American aspiration. He contributed more than
military ability and statesmanship; he also contributed his
character and charisma to the cause—and by force of
personality carried many Americans along with him to
victory.

Leaving Philadelphia immediately upon his appointment,
he set out for Boston. As he traveled, battles were occurring.
On the night of June 16-17, a patriot force of 1,200 men were
sent to seize Bunker Hill, one of the heights surrounding
Boston in anticipation that General Gage would try to occupy
it. The Americans occupied and fortified Breed's Hill nearer to
Boston, and on the morning of June 17 were attacked by
three thousand British troops. Twice the Americans repulsed
charges, but with a third attempt the British took the hill. In
the effort, however, they lost 1,054 men to American losses
of 449. Despite the loss of Breed's Hill, the Americans were
inspired by their showing for the fight to come. Also inspiring
the troops was word that Ethan Allen and Benedict Arnold,
with only 83 men, had taken Fort Ticonderoga on Lake
Champlain on May 10. Thus when Washington arrived and
took command on July 3, his 14,500 men were in high spirits.

Early in the war a principal American objective was

"Pulling Down the Statue of George III by the 'Sons of Freedom'"
(Engraving by John McRae, 1859, after a painting by Johannes A. Oertel)

Canada. The Continental Congress on May 29, 1775, had issued an address to "fellow sufferers" in Canada inviting them to join the rebellion—which Canadians largely failed to heed, for the Quebec Act had pacified them. On November 8 General Benedict Arnold with six hundred men reached Quebec after marching through Maine and laid siege. Five days later General Richard Montgomery captured Montreal, then moved immediately to join Arnold at Quebec. On December 31 the two forces together assaulted Quebec; Montgomery was killed, the attack failed, and Arnold was forced to retreat the following spring to Fort Ticonderoga. These moves did alarm England sufficiently for its military strategists to send a large force there.

Washington's siege of Boston ended more happily for the American cause than the attempt to conquer Canada. On March 17, Sir William Howe (who had succeeded Gage in command) abandoned the city by sailing for Halifax. He intended to move from Halifax on New York City. Washington anticipated this move and between April and August, 1776, moved from Boston to New York. There he had troops numbering approximately 33,000. Howe did arrive with 34,000 men, and on August 27 the two forces fought the Battle of Long Island. The Americans were defeated and Washington retreated, evacuating Long Island for Manhattan on August 29-30. Defeated again, Washington retreated to Hackensack, New Jersey, intent on Fabian tactics. He would fight no major battle in which his army might be defeated, but retreat, fight small actions, and retreat until the British army was worn down.

On December 11, Washington was forced by Lord Cornwallis to cross the Delaware River into Pennsylvania, whereupon the British troops went into winter quarters. The American general knew that his situation was desperate; his supplies were low, and his troops were dwindling away. To the Continental Congress, Washington wrote of his needs, stating that he must have more men and more material aid or else "the game will be pretty much up." Even the ringing words of Nathan Hale as he went to the gallows as a spy, "I regret that I have but one life to give for my country," did not electrify the young nation. Nor did Thomas Paine's pamphlet,

"Valley Forge, 1777, Gen. Washington & Lafayette visiting the suffering Part of the Army" (from a painting by A. Gilbert)

"Washington Crossing the Alleheny River" (engraving by D. Kimberly for Columbian Magazine)

The American Crisis, stimulate a wave of enlistments; his sentence in the work, "These are the times that try men's souls," was most appropriate. A time of trial was ahead. Aiding the American cause far more than words was Washington's brilliant counterattack late that year. On Christmas night, 1776, he recrossed the Delaware to attack the Hessian garrison at Trenton on December 26, killing many of them and capturing two thousand. Then on January 3, 1777, he fought the Battle of Princeton in New Jersey, defeating Lord Cornwallis, before going into winter quarters near Morristown, New Jersey.

In March 1777 the British Secretary of State, Lord Germain, approved an overall strategy for the war: a three-pronged attack to divide the colonies. One British column was to invade New York from Canada by way of Lake Champlain; another column was to slash into New York from Lake Ontario by way of the Mohawk Valley; and Lord Howe was to drive from New York City and seize Philadelphia. Only one aspect of this plan succeeded. Lord Howe landed fifteen thousand troops at the head of Chesapeake Bay to find Washington and 10,500 men blocking the road to Philadelphia. On September 11, Howe defeated Washington at the Battle of Brandywine Creek in Pennsylvania, then slipped around the Americans and occupied Philadelphia at the end of that month.

Elsewhere the British master plan failed. Colonel Barry St. Leger, leading the British force from Lake Ontario, was forced to retire by the timely actions of Benedict Arnold in late August. General John Burgoyne, moving down the Lake Champlain route from Canada, fought a series of engagements collectively known as the Battle of Saratoga between September 19 and October 17. Near Freeman's Farm at Bemis Heights, Burgoyne suffered heavy losses first to General Horatio Gates and then to Benedict Arnold. On October 17, Burgoyne surrendered with 5,700 men to General Gates. Meanwhile, Washington was moving into winter quarters at Valley Forge, there to suffer from shortages of food and supplies during the extreme cold. To the British it seemed strange that the colonial troops could endure the bitter conditions of Valley Forge. Some seemed to

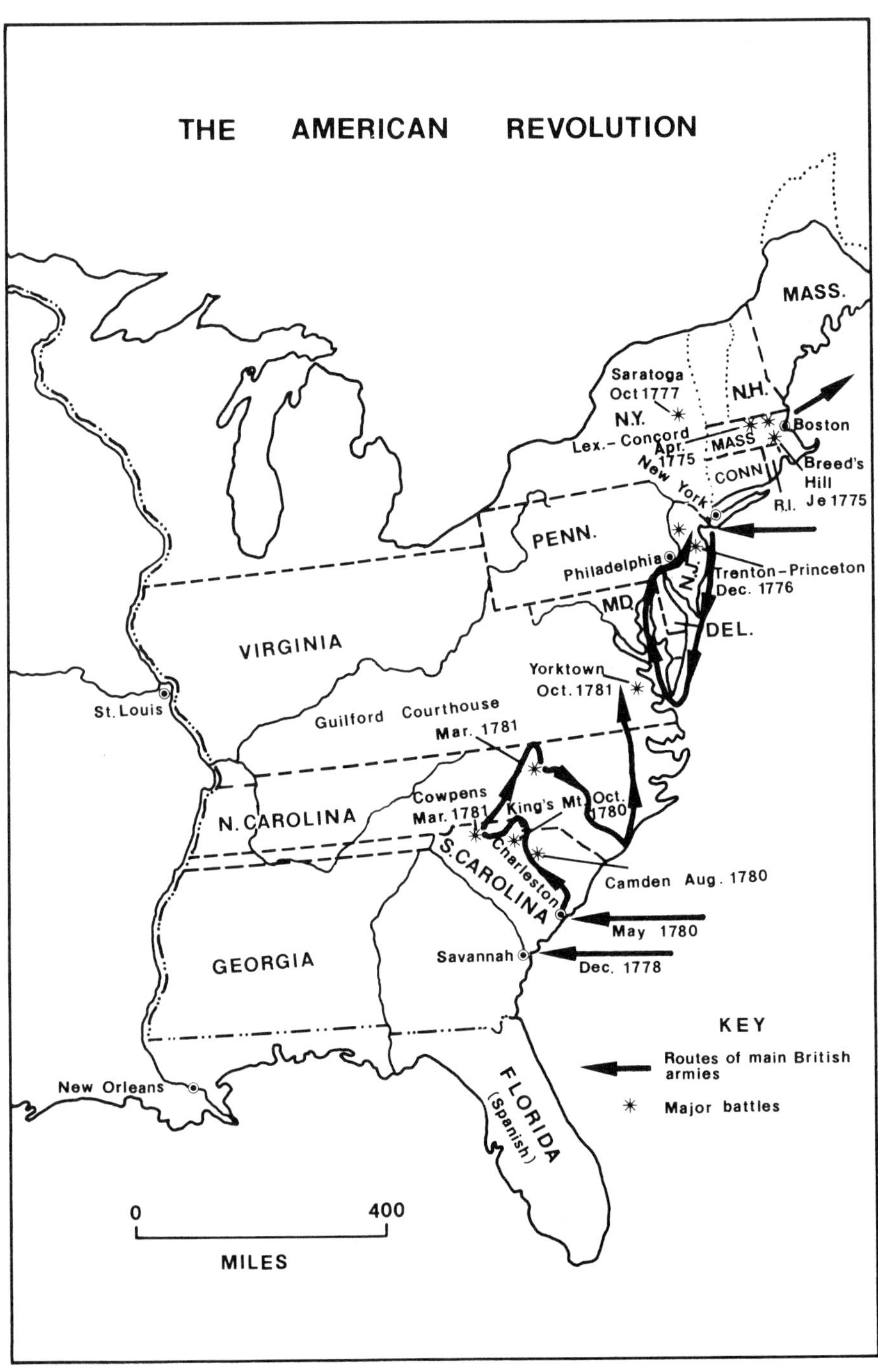

THE AMERICAN REVOLUTION
MASS.
Saratoga
Oct 1777
N.H.
N.Y.
Lex.- Concord
Apr. 1775
MASS
CONN
Boston
Breed's
Hill
Je 1775
R.I.
New York
PENN.
Philadelphia
N.J.
Trenton-Princeton
Dec. 1776
MD.
DEL.
VIRGINIA
Yorktown
Oct. 1781
St. Louis
Guilford Courthouse
Mar. 1781
Cowpens
Mar. 1781
King's Mt
Oct.
1780
N. CAROLINA
S. CAROLINA
Charleston
Camden Aug. 1780
May 1780
GEORGIA
Savannah
Dec. 1778
KEY
Routes of main British
armies
Major battles
New Orleans
FLORIDA
(Spanish)
0
400
MILES

think the men endured because of loyalty to George
Washington. But had they read the Declaration of
Independence closely, they would have realized that the
American soldiers were fighting not for a man nor yet for a
nation; rather they were fighting for an idea, one which
Thomas Jefferson had captured in words when he wrote *"that
all men are created equal"* and "that they are endowed by their
Creator with certain unalienable Rights, that among these are
Life, Liberty and the pursuit of Happiness." The soldiers at
Valley Forge were one with Patrick Henry, who had stated
that life was not yet so sweet as to be bought at the price of
chains and slavery. And so these soldiers endured, although
to them it perhaps seemed that the American cause was ill-
fated.

Suddenly, however, came news of the Battle of Saratoga,
an engagement that changed the course of the war. A report
of this American victory, when it arrived on the Continent,
led French and Spanish generals to think the Americans had a
chance of victory—and therefore merited French and Spanish
aid. In 1778 France declared war on England, and Spain soon
made a similar decision. French volunteers, the French fleet,
Spanish supplies, and the diversion of war in Europe took
sufficient pressure off the Americans to enable them to
continue the struggle.

This European aid was secured through the diplomatic
efforts of Silas Deane, Arthur Lee, and Benjamin Franklin.
On March 4, 1778, Congress ratified the result of their
efforts, a treaty with France providing an alliance between
the two nations stating that neither nation would make peace
without consulting the other. The American Navy profited
greatly from this arrangement; soon ships outfitted in France
were attacking British coastal towns, while John Paul Jones
used French ports as a base for his fights with British men-of-
war. French noblemen, such as the Marquis de Lafayette,
gave prestige to the colonial army by their presence with
Washington, as did Baron Friedrich Wilhelm von Steuben and
Thaddeus Kosciusko.

Equally noteworthy was the Spanish contribution from
Louisiana. Governor Bernardo De Gálvez seized eleven
English vessels at New Orleans. He also sold needed supplies
to the Americans at Fort Pitt and other frontier posts. From

New Orleans came the weapons and ammunition that enabled George Rogers Clark to fight the British and the Indians in the Illinois country. Gálvez invaded East and West Florida, capturing Mobile in March, 1780, and the following year secured Pensacola, thereby making Florida Spanish once again. The British grew tired of this Spanish bother and determined on an expedition down the Mississippi from Canada; it was to take St. Louis, reconquer Illinois, and make contact with British troops in Florida. Captain Emmanuel Hesse therefore gathered some one thousand soldiers and Indian allies and moved on St. Louis. However, Captain Fernando de Leyba, commanding at St. Louis, frustrated the plan; with only three hundred soldiers and militia he fought so vigorously on May 26, 1780, that the attackers grew discouraged and retired northward. Thus Spanish aid diverted British soldiers to Florida, enabled George Rogers Clark to hold the old Northwest Territory for Americans, and frustrated British plans to link Canada and Florida by way of the Mississippi River.

Meanwhile, Lord Howe in May, 1778, was supplanted as commander of British forces by General Henry Clinton. His orders were to evacuate Philadelphia and move to New York City. When Clinton began this move, Washington followed him across New Jersey, and on June 28 they fought the inconclusive Battle of Monmouth, which ended in a draw that allowed Clinton to enter New York City. Washington followed and encamped at White Plains to keep watch.

The major thrust of the war then swung southward. British strategists felt they could count on heavy Loyalist support to conquer the southern colonies. Under Clinton's planning, Savannah, Georgia, was taken in December 1778 and Georgia shortly was overrun. Clinton personally led a force, going by ship from New York, that on May 12, 1780, took Charleston, South Carolina, along with five thousand American prisoners. Clinton then departed for New York, leaving Cornwallis in charge. In July, Cornwallis moved northward, and on August 16 he inflicted a crushing defeat on the Americans under General Gates at Camden, South Carolina. However, as this army marched into North Carolina, it suffered a defeat at King's Mountain on October

7, 1780, forcing Cornwallis back into South Carolina. Then on January 16, 1781, Cornwallis was defeated again at Cowpens, South Carolina, by an American force led by General Daniel Morgan. Cornwallis thereupon decided to move northward into Virginia; with 1,500 troops he marched, raiding villages and farms along the way, to take up a position at Yorktown on August 1, 1781, his army increasing to approximately 8,000 men. He believed that the British navy could evacuate him should that become necessary. He failed to realize that the British navy was concentrated at Jamaica, fearing a French attack there.

George Washington learned that a French fleet of twenty vessels under Admiral de Grasse had chosen to sail to Yorktown, not Jamaica. Therefore, he and the French commander, the Comte de Rochambeau, gave up their plan to attack New York City and led their troops southward. With the aid of the French fleet, they assembled an army of 16,000 troops at Williamsburg and on September 28 began the Siege of Yorktown. Three weeks later, on October 19, Cornwallis surrendered more than seven thousand troops to Washington while the American band played a march called, "The World Turned Upside Down." Lord North, upon hearing the news, cried out, "Oh God! it is all over!" He resigned the ministry in March 1782, and the Marquis of Rockingham formed a government that would negotiate a treaty of peace.

Attempts to settle the war diplomatically were the province of the Continental Congress, which had remained in session throughout the war. It had established a Committee for Foreign Affairs on April 17, 1777, which was responsible for sending agents to Europe to secure aid from other nations. England had responded to the prodding of prominent citizens by naming a British Peace Commission under Lord Carlisle on April 12, 1778; this commission actually spent that summer and fall in America, but had been unsuccessful in bringing peace. Then in 1779 Congress on November 3 appointed John Adams to negotiate peace with England. In June 1781, Franklin and John Jay became part of a peace commission with Adams; Thomas Jefferson also was named to the committee, but declined to serve. The commission made little headway until 1782 when on March 4 the House of Commons voted to end the war in America and on March 22 the Rockingham ministry assumed office. On April 12 the British dispatched Richard Oswald to Paris to begin talks with Franklin. After seven years of warfare, serious negotiating began.

The treaty that resulted a year and a half later was favorable to the United States largely through the efforts of Benjamin Franklin. Strangely, the American enemies at the conference were the French and Spanish diplomats, not the English. Spain had never recognized American independence, and it did not want the Americans to gain the Mississippi River as a western boundary; instead the Spanish envoys were seeking to have the old Northwest Territory retained by England and to have Alabama, Mississippi, and parts of Kentucky and Tennessee ceded to Spain. Benjamin Franklin, in separate negotiations with England, pointed out the British advantages to an amicable parting with its former colonies, and thus separate treaties resulted. On January 20, 1783, England signed treaties with France and Spain that saw Florida given to Spain. Then on September 3 came the Peace of Paris between England and the United States that settled differences between the two nations.

A view of Independence Hall in Philadelphia

One Government or Thirteen?

On June 7, 1776—the same day it accepted a motion to declare the independence of the country—the Second Continental Congress voted another committee into existence, this one charged with drafting a plan for a central government for the united colonies. The delegates in Philadelphia realized that in the midst of war unity was necessary, for no one colony could wage the conflict to a successful conclusion; victory required concerted action. This fact was widely recognized, for at every crisis of the past century the colonies had moved toward unity.

As early as 1643, when the colonies of New England had been threatened by the Indians and the Dutch, the New England Confederation had been organized. The best-known attempt at unity had come in 1754 when the Albany Congress convened; this meeting had been called to formulate a concerted plan to meet the threat posed by the French in Canada and their Indian allies. Benjamin Franklin, who had been there as a delegate from Pennsylvania, suggested to the other delegates, who represented Maryland, New York, and New England, that they should adopt a "Plan of Union," which called for uniting the colonies under a President-General appointed by the King. A council of delegates from the colonies would be established with the power to legislate on matters of intercolonial interest, to tax, to raise armies, and to negotiate with the Indians, but the power of veto was to be reserved to the President-General and the Crown. Matters of intercolonial interest, as Franklin saw them in 1754, included the administration and disposal of western

John Dickinson

lands, the right to declare war and make peace, and to govern
the frontier regions beyond the boundaries of the colonies;
local matters would be reserved to the individual colonies.
Franklin's plan proved too bold in 1754; the colonial
legislatures rejected it because they were loath to relinquish
any of their powers to any "national" government and
because land speculators, who preferred to deal with local
governments, were strongly against it. Moreover, the British
Parliament rejected the plan because its members feared
rising colonial democratic tendencies.

Other attempts at colonial unity had included the Stamp
Act Congress of 1765, the Committees of Correspondence,
and even the First Continental Congress of 1774. However,
none of these had been able to function as a "national"
government, for each colony jealously guarded its individual
rights. Yet the emergency of 1776 was so great that the
delegates to that Second Continental Congress knew they
had to formulate some workable plan of union, one which
would be able to prosecute the war, win peace, and stabilize
relations between the individual colonies. These thoughtful
men gathered in Philadelphia that June of 1776 knew that
after their war for independence was won, some type of
national government was necessary to regulate trade between
the colonies, control the western lands, and limit the amount
of paper money that could be issued by the states.

John Dickinson, a delegate from Pennsylvania, was
appointed that seventh day of June in 1776 to head the
committee to draft a plan for some type of national
government. Born in 1732 in Maryland, he had moved as a
youngster to Dover, Delaware, where his father had a large
estate. There he was educated by private tutor. At the age of
eighteen he went to study in the offices of John Moland, a
prominent Philadelphia lawyer; then in 1753 he journeyed to
London to study law at the Middle Temple. Returning to
Philadelphia in 1757, he began practicing his profession. His
rise to prominence among colonial leaders thereafter was
rapid. In 1760 he was elected to the Assembly of Delaware
and became the speaker; two years later, at the same time
that he was arguing cases before the supreme court of the
colony of Pennsylvania, he was elected a representative from

Philadelphia to the colonial legislature there. A staunch
conservative, Dickinson in the two years that followed would
argue against ending the proprietary status of the colony of
Pennsylvania, stating that any government appointed by the
British ministry would be far worse than that inflicted by the
proprietary owners. His stance proved unpopular, and in 1765
he failed to be reelected to his seat.

Losing interest in the legal profession, he chose to study
history and politics—and to make his feelings known on
political issues by his writings. In 1765, when the Sugar and
Stamp Acts were rousing passions in America, he published
*The Late Regulations Respecting the British Colonies . . .*in which he
argued that Americans needed to enlist the aid of English
merchants in their fight; he stated his belief that these
merchants would join with Americans if they saw that their
own economic interests were threatened by the Sugar and
Stamp Acts. As a result of this pamphlet—and of his obvious
knowledge on the subject—he was appointed one of
Pennsylvania's delegates to the Stamp Act Congress of
October 1765.

In the years that followed he published his opinions and
thoughts—and reasoning—on each of the items of
controversy between England and the colonies. These
appeared anonymously in the *Pennsylvania Chronicle*; later they
were gathered into a pamphlet called *Letters from a Farmer in
Pennsylvania to the Inhabitants of the British Colonies*. In these essays
he argued that British policy of the day was evil, that force
might be the ultimate necessity, but that conciliation still was
possible. Because of the obvious deep knowledge of the
British constitutional system and of traditional British
liberties shown in the *Letters* , Dickinson was widely honored;
for example, he was thanked at a public meeting in Boston
and was awarded an honorary doctorate of laws by Princeton
University.

Throughout this troubled era, Dickinson supported the
Patriot cause, but always as an opponent of force condemning
the hotheads of New England. For example, in 1774 when
actions in Boston brought a crisis that led the local citizens
there to request aid from the other colonies, Dickinson was
opposed to giving anything other than an expression of

sympathy; yet simultaneously he was chairman of the
Committee of Correspondence in Philadelphia. A member of
the First Continental Congress, he drafted the appeal to the
people of Canada and the petition to the king proposing
reconciliation. In the Second Continental Congress, it was he
who drafted the petition to George III suggesting a peaceful
settlement to the growing quarrel—just as it was he who
drafted the "Declaration of the Causes of taking up Arms."

Dickinson was a study in contradictions. He would vote
against the Declaration of Independence, yet he was but one
of two members of Congress who would take up arms to
fight for the measures for which they had been voting.
Dickinson was keenly aware of the potential of the
Revolution growing into a social war in America, something
he did not want. He, as well as other conservative Patriots,
wanted to halt the tendency toward royal absolutism in
England; they wanted to retain the traditional British liberties
and the rights of self-government which the colonies had
been exercising. But they did not want a social revolution in
America, one which would sweep the lower classes into
positions of leadership.

This fear on Dickinson's part was based on his
observation of past events and on his study of colonial
history. During the settlement of most of the colonies, the
pioneers who moved to the western frontier found they were
not allowed representatives in the legislative bodies in
proportion to their growing numbers; thus they believed—
and with good reason—that they were discriminated against
by the minority of landed wealthy people in the east. These
western settlers, who were exposed to danger from the
Indians, believed that the legislative bodies were not affording
them adequate military protection. Members of
fundamentalist religious sects, they often resented the church
supported by the colony. They objected to the tax structure
voted by the eastern planters and merchants. Feeling
discriminated against, they hated their creditors and the land
speculators to whom they always seemed to be in debt. These
same frontiersmen were gaining the franchise, for they did
own land—and land (or other forms of property) was the
basis for gaining the right to vote. People such as John

Dickinson therefore saw their monopoly on positions of
leadership being challenged by this new majority—and
naturally feared it.

Dickinson therefore, in drafting his Articles of
Confederation, sought to prevent the war with England from
becoming a social as well as political revolution. His desire
was to create a strong central government, one capable of
keeping the majority under the continued rule of the
minority. His draft, presented to Congress on July 12, 1776,
called for a Congress in which each state would have one
vote; this vote was to be cast by a delegation whose members
were elected by the legislature in each state—and no delegate
could serve more than three years out of six. The Articles did
give the federal government real power; the states retained
only the power to control their internal policy—but only if
this did not interfere with the national government. The only
restriction on the Congress was that it could not levy duties
except to maintain a post office. It would control the western
lands, the armed forces, conduct foreign affairs, negotiate
with the Indians, and arbitrate disputes between the states. In
short, it contained few limitations on the powers of the
federal government while severely restricting the powers of
the states.

During a month of debate about the document which
Dickinson had drafted, many objections surfaced. First—and
perhaps foremost—there was no possibility that the states
would agree to a constitution creating a government superior
to themselves. In this debate about where sovereignty really
resided—in the states or at the national level—popular
sentiment was on the side of those opposed to a strong
central government. Residents in each state, in fact, in almost
each county, saw themselves as separate from other parts of
the country; each locality had separate social, political,
economic, and religious attitudes. A man's country was his
state, no more; for example, John Adams referred to the
congressional delegation as "our embassy." Therefore the
delegates added Article II to the document drafted by
Dickinson, one which stated that *each state retains its sovereignty,
freedom, and independence, and every power, jurisdiction, and right which
is not by this confederation expressly delegated to the United States in*

Congress assembled." In short, the states would be supreme, not
the central government.

Tied to this same vexing question was the debate about
representation in the Congress. The First and Second
Continental Congresses had allowed each state one vote, and
Dickinson had agreed. However, the states with large
populations—Massachusetts, Pennsylvania, and Virginia—
insisted that votes in the Congress should be apportioned on
the basis of population; the more people in a state, the greater
should be its vote in Congress. This, they argued, would be
more truly representational government. Naturally the
smaller states (in terms of population) disagreed, arguing that
the new government was a confederation of equally free and
equally sovereign states, each of which should be allowed an
equal vote. Joining with the small state delegates were those
who wanted to keep the new central government subordinate
to the individual states; these individuals wanted no central
government representing the people, but rather one that
represented the states. In the end the "small state" delegates
had their way; each state under the Articles would have one
vote.

The second major argument came over how the central
government would be financed and exactly how much each
state was to contribute to the central treasury. Dickinson had
proposed that money should be raised within each state based
on population. Delegates from those states where slavery was
legal argued that slaves should not be counted in making such
assessments; rather the value of the land within each state
should be the basis of taxation. Delegates from northern
states objected violently. In the end the two sides
compromised, and the final draft of the Articles provided that
the expenses of the central government would be shared by
the states on the basis of located and improved lands in each
state.

Finally, and most hotly debated, was the issue of control
of the western lands. Some of the states, such as Maryland
and Pennsylvania, had definite western limits, while others,
such as Virginia and Georgia, laid claim to almost unlimited
numbers of acres in the west. In this the landed states
prevailed; a provision was inserted in the proposed Articles

that no state could be deprived of its territory without its consent.

In the end the powers of the central government were sharply limited and clearly spelled out: it controlled foreign affairs, declaring war and concluding treaties; it had the power to raise armies and build a navy; it managed relations with the various Indian tribes; it could coin and borrow money; and it could operate a post office. All acts of Congress required the approval of nine of the thirteen states, but no amendments could be made to the Articles without the unanimous consent of all the states. This central government could not collect taxes; its funds were to be voted by the individual states. Inasmuch as this government had no chief executive and no system of courts, there was no way to enforce any of its laws or punish any who violated its powers.

The debate ended in August of 1776 with no final action. The matter came before the Continental Congress again the following April, and the Articles were finally ratified on November 15, 1777. Two days later they were sent to the individual states for acceptance—and all had to accept them before they would become effective.

Ratification of the Articles moved smoothly at first. By July of 1778, eight states had agreed to them. The stumbling block for the rest proved to be the western land claims. New Jersey, Delaware, and Maryland refused to agree to the Articles until all states ceded their claims to the central government. The Maryland resolution summed up the feeling in these three states: the war was a common effort and the western lands should be a common heritage "subject to be parcelled by Congress into free, convenient and independent governments." In September of 1780 the Congress asked those states with land claims in the west to surrender these to the central government. New York led the way with a cession that same year, and Virginia, which had the largest and strongest claim, followed in January of 1781. Thereupon Maryland, the last state to accept them, ratified the articles in February, and on March 1 the government was proclaimed in effect. Robert Livingston became Secretary of Foreign Affairs and Robert Morris the Superintendent of Finance. Government under the Articles of Confederation had begun just at the time that the Revolution itself came to a successful conclusion at Yorktown.

Although this government would prove weak and ineffective, it was a beginning—and a major one—toward forming a nation of thirteen diverse states. Montesquieu had written that republican government was possible only in a small homogeneous society whose interests were extremely similar; in the United States of 1781 there was North and South, East and West, tidewater and backcountry, slavery and freedom. The Articles did bring these together in some form of harmony, for they provided that each state had to give "full faith and credit" to the acts of other states, that each state was required to extend its privileges and immunities to free citizens of the other states, that individual citizens could move freely with their goods from one state to another, and that all states would act in concert in matters of war and peace.

Yet the immediate tendency following the Revolution was toward fragmentation. The hatred of a powerful English government had not inclined the Patriots in America to sympathy toward a strong central government in their own land. Even the words of pamphleteer Thomas Paine had little immediate effect; his last issue of *The American Crisis*, dated April 19, 1783, stated, "Sovereignty must have power to protect all the parts that compose and constitute it; and as UNITED STATES we are equal to the importance of the title, but otherwise we are not. Our Union, well and wisely regulated and cemented, is the cheapest way of being great— the easiest way of being powerful, and the happiest invention in government which the circumstances of America can admit of." No such cement was available, however, for the states were wandering apart, not drawing closer together.

During the war years—at the same time they were debating and accepting the Articles of Confederation—the various states had been drafting constitutions as recommended by the Continental Congress. In these they had put into practice the theory that government is of the people, for the people, and by the people, resting on the consent of the governed, and given solid form in a written constitution. During the war the "compact theory"—the idea that the people together form by consent a written organ of government—had been poorly practiced; the difficulties of war made it almost impossible for the voters to ratify the constitutions that were written. In some states, such as New Hampshire, Georgia, Delaware, New York, and Vermont, the legislatures had ratified the constitutions. In others, such as Pennsylvania, Maryland, and North Carolina, the constitutions had been framed by constitutional conventions but had not been submitted to the people for acceptance or rejection. Only Massachusetts followed what would be called the modern process: a constitutional convention wrote the document in 1780 and then it was ratified by the people (in 1784 New Hampshire's constitution also would be ratified by popular vote).

These state constitutions, so diverse in origin, did have a remarkable similarity. They showed the impact of the democratic principles that had motivated the war; they contained bills of rights, provided for elected legislatures (bicameral except in Pennsylvania) that would be strong through control of the fiscal power, allowed the governors little real power, and called for frequent elections. Yet despite the democratic feelings evident in these documents, there were property qualifications for voting in every state except one, all designed to keep government in the hands of the wealthy class, and in most states there also were religious qualifications, especially some designed to keep Roman Catholics from holding office. In short, the framers of these constitutions for the most part subscribed to the theory that the body politic was constituted of those with a stake in society.

In many states there were social and economic concessions to democracy. Virginia in 1776 had passed a call for "free exercise of religion" to allow freedom of conscience to all citizens with no restrictions on holding public office. When the Revolutionary War began, there was an established church in nine of the thirteen colonies—Congregationalism in all the colonies of New England except Rhode Island, and the Anglican Church in six other colonies. Only Pennsylvania and Rhode Island had anything approaching freedom of religion. After the Revolution, however, toleration became more widespread.

Another change was the abolition of slavery through gradual emancipation in Pennsylvania, Connecticut, Rhode Island, New Jersey, and New York by 1786, while the importation of slaves had ended in all states save South Carolina and Georgia by that year. This change was due, in part, to the humanitarianism of the leaders of the new republic—leaders who sincerely believed that "all men are created equal"—and, in part, to religious beliefs that held slavery to be wrong. Even in Virginia, where slavery had long been practiced, the state legislature urged the gradual freeing of slaves—and within less than ten years some 10,000 slaves had been freed there.

Another change growing out of the Revolution was the attitude about the public lands owned by the various states. All the states needed money with which to pay the costs of the Revolution, and these acres might have been sold to speculators to raise the funds needed, or they might have been leased to provide a long-range income. Instead these lands generally were used to pay the past-due salaries of soldiers who had fought in the Revolution, thereby increasing the number of land-holding citizens—and participants in government. There also were changes to abolish primogeniture and entailed estates; these laws were long-range in effect, gradually breaking up large estates. Under the new state constitutions, debtors and prisoners were better treated than they had been under the English common law.

Yet these new state constitutions, along with the national government provided by the Articles, did not bring about a revolution such as France would undergo a few years later (or Russia in the twentieth century). The basic structure of society was not altered in the United States; the revolution was principally political, not social. True those who supported the British in the late war, the Loyalists, had been impoverished or driven out of the country, but the Patriots who were wealthy became just as conservative as the Loyalists had been.

Yes, Americans in 1783 could celebrate their freedom from England. Yet within just four short years they learned that freedom brought responsibilities and the need for self-discipline, a concept that seemingly must be relearned by each generation. They had fought against taxation—and then had to tax themselves. They had fought against the burdens of government—and then had to govern themselves. They had fought against the invasion of their individual rights—and then in the name of the "general good" had to place restrictions on their individual rights. They quickly were made to realize that the world is one of reality, not of theory, that freedom belongs only to the responsible and strong, not the weak and undisciplined, and that freedom is costly, not free. The nation would survive this time of trial—though not without turmoil—because of one difference between the old order and the new: their taxes, their governmental burdens, and their restrictions on individual liberties were self-imposed by men of vision who truly believed in democracy, not by a tyrant bent on enlarging his own power.

In 1783, when the treaty whereby the English recognized American independence finally was signed, the most pressing problem facing the national government created by the Articles of Confederation was a shortage of money—as it would be in the years that followed. On January 25 that year Congress proved unable to satisfy the claims of the officers of the Continental Army for back pay. The bulk of George Washington's troops were at Newburg on the Hudson, and the officers and men there did not want to disband until they had been paid, for their salaries were greatly in arrears. Moreover, the officers of this army had been promised half-pay for life, and they wished this matter to be arranged. In December of 1782 they had drafted a threat to take the matter into their own hands if Congress did not arrange to pay them. As on January 25 Congress admitted it was unable to do so, discontent continued to grow. In March a second threat appeared, this one in the form of an anonymous manifesto largely the work of a leader of the dissident officers, Major John Armstrong. This paper urged the soldiers not to disband and called for a meeting of all officers for the following day. George Washington, upon hearing of this paper, called his own meeting—and at it spoke so eloquently against actions which would disgrace the army and the country that he "drew tears from many of the officers." He promised the men his best efforts in their behalf whereupon, when he withdrew, the officers voted a resolution expressing their faith in the justice of Congress and denouncing the anonymous circular. Washington had prevented a mutiny, but he could not help Congress out of its financial difficulties.

In April that year the members of the Congress decided to put the funding of the central government on a legal basis. They did this by proposing the so-called Revenue Amendment to the Articles of Confederation. Under the terms of this proposed amendment, an import tax was to be laid on goods entering the United States for a period of twenty-five years, and $1,500,000 was to be raised annually through requisitions on the states according to population rather than on the value of land. This measure failed to carry by a wide margin; within three years only two states had accepted it while seven had agreed to it in part and four ignored it. Thereupon Congress issued an urgent appeal to the states, pointing out its own financial plight; twelve states then ratified the amendment—but New York's negative vote killed the measure, for the unanimous consent of all the states was necessary to ratify any change in the Articles.

In its first five years of existence, 1781 to 1786, Congress received just less than $2,500,000 through requisitions to the states—and that was trickling to a virtual halt; in the fourteen months prior to January 1, 1786, these donations had fallen to a rate of less than $375,000 per year—far less than was needed for the operation of the central government. Congress had been reduced to issuing paper money backed only by faith that someday the government would be able to redeem it in gold or silver. For a short time this faith was evident and the currency did hold its value; then it began to shrink rapidly—whereupon Congress printed yet more of it and it declined even further. Eventually a thousand Continental dollars were worth about one dollar in specie. Congress did secure a loan from Holland that kept it from failing altogether to meet its obligations, but always it was facing imminent bankruptcy.

This inability to pay its obligations led to extreme Congressional embarrassment. In June of 1783 some eighty disgruntled members of the Pennsylvania militia, unhappy at poor treatment and lack of pay, marched to Philadelphia under command of their non-commissioned officers and demanded that Congress help them. Drinking at nearby pubs brought such unruly acts from these militiamen that the members of Congress appealed to Pennsylvania authorities for protection. When this was refused, the members of Congress on June 24 fled to Princeton, New Jersey, and later to Annapolis, Maryland. Not only were they unable to pay these militiamen, but also they could not find the money to pay the interest on the public debt. So few members of Congress were in attendance that a quorum could rarely be raised to take any action on any matter. Washington did prevail on the army to disband in June of 1783 because Congress had promised to pay the soldiers in warrants good for western land; thereby a military coup was prevented. Eventually the central government came to rest in New York City, which was declared the temporary national capital.

The government under the Articles of Confederation failed just as miserably in the field of foreign affairs as it had in fiscal matters. The people of the United States, ninety-five percent of them, were engaged in agriculture of one type or another, and they desperately needed foreign markets for their produce. During the war itself, when Spain and France had been allies, the farmers had secured high prices for their output, and prosperity had resulted. After the conflict ended, however, Spain and France largely revoked the trading concessions they had granted. And British Orders in Council closed the West Indies to American shipping after May 1783, thereby halting yet another profitable source of trade.

The members of Congress searched desperately for some way to force favorable trade treaties with European powers, for the outraged—and financially troubled—citizens of all the states were demanding action. The answer seemed to be the same that had worked with British merchants during the protests over the Sugar and Tea Acts: commercial retaliation. Some way had to be found to hurt European merchants so they, in turn, would bring pressure to bear on their governments. Moreover, because the United States presented the spectacle of a nation virtually without a central government, the British were refusing to abandon their trading posts in the old Northwest Territory; thereby they were securing for themselves the valuable fur trade. This they intended to do until, as they thought, the United States would collapse into anarchy and ask for a return of British rule. All attempts by officials of the national government to negotiate with European powers failed except minor agreements with Sweden and Prussia; the reason for this failure was made known to John Adams, ambassador to England, when he was asked contemptuously if he was trying to negotiate "One treaty, or thirteen?"

Congress in 1784 sought the necessary power from the states, prefacing the request with the statement that "The fortune of every Citizen is interested in the success" of such negotiations. All Americans needed a resumption of the commerce that had brought wealth to the United States. "Unless the United States in Congress assembled shall be vested with powers competent to the protection of commerce, they can never command reciprocal advantages in trade," related this request. The proposal stated that Congress should be granted the power for fifteen years to prohibit the importing or exporting of goods from American ports unless these moved in ships owned by Americans—or in ships belonging to foreign governments that had trade treaties with the United States. Only two states bothered to agree. The rest ignored it.

The inability of the central government to secure commercial concessions from foreign powers led the states to begin commercial warfare on one another as each sought profits for its own citizens. They erected tariff barriers against each other, as well as engaging in petty boundary disputes. The result was thirteen virtually independent states rather than "United States."

The impotence of the central government led Spain to dabble in sedition on the American frontier. Spanish officials hoped to secure the territory between the Appalachian Mountains and the Mississippi River and between the Ohio River and the Gulf of Mexico. From forts in East and West Florida, Spaniards urged Indians under American jurisdiction to war against the citizens of the new Republic, and the American right of transit on the Mississippi River, guaranteed by treaty with Spain, was openly violated.

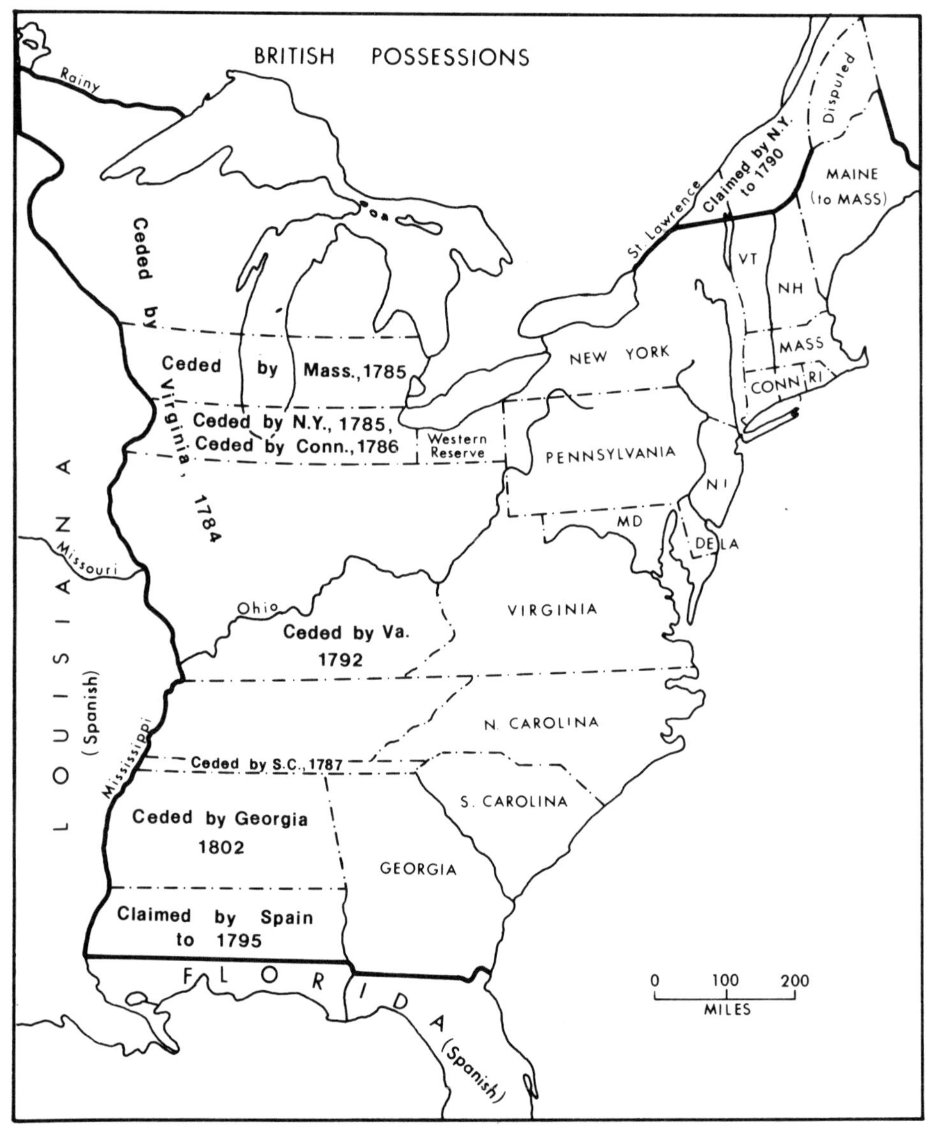

CESSION OF WESTERN LANDS

Frontiersmen in Tennessee and Kentucky were prevented
from floating their goods down the river to New Orleans, the
easiest way to transport them to Europe or the cities along
the Atlantic Coast. Spanish money was given to selected
individuals in that region for the purpose of financing
secession from the United States and the annexation to Spain.
John Jay, Secretary for Foreign Affairs, negotiated with the
Spanish ambassador to the United States, Diego de Gardoqui,
and produced a proposed treaty that would have surrendered
the American claim to the right of navigation on the
Mississippi for twenty-five years in return for a favorable
reception of American ships in Spanish ports. However, this
treaty failed to win passage in Congress because the delegates
from Southern states were more interested in the river than
in trade with Spain.

One major success of the Congress was its handling of
the western lands. This need came to its attention due to the
problems caused by the disorderly settlement of Kentucky
and Tennessee. Two speculators from Virginia, John Sevier
and James Robertson, had taken frontiersmen into the
Watauga and Holston rivers region in the 1770s, while Daniel
Boone had blazed his Wilderness Road into Kentucky for the
Transylvania Company in January of 1775. Settlers had
continued to flock to that region during the Revolution. By
1784 there were some 10,000 people there, periodically
fighting the Cherokees, and on August 23, 1784, they had
self-organized the state of Franklin (in present Tennessee).
Other would-be states were organized at local initiative in
Kentucky by the Transylvania Company and in the
Cumberland Valley by James Robertson. Internal strife,
Indian wars, and conflicts for leadership tore all three
projected states to the extent that George Washington on a
visit to the region in 1784 was appalled. To avoid the
repetition of this situation, he urged the Congress to provide
for the orderly settlement of the West.

In 1785 a Northwest Ordinance—largely written by
Thomas Jefferson—was passed. This ordinance provided for
the orderly survey and sale of land in the Northwest
Territory. It stated that as new tracts of land were opened to
settlement, these would be surveyed into townships each six

miles square and thus consisting of thirty-six sections of land. Four sections in every township were to be reserved for the government and another section to pay for maintaining a public school. The other thirty-one sections were to be sold at public auction to be held at convenient locations, with the minimum price of one dollar per acre in cash. However, it quickly became evident that the basic price of $640 for the minimum amount of land at the lowest possible price was discouraging actual settlers, while the dollar-per-acre price was discouraging speculators from purchasing large tracts. Therefore Congress passed a special act allowing the purchase of 1,500,000 acres at nine cents per acre by a group that organized as the Ohio Company; it, in turn—and at a profit—began selling small amounts to actual settlers.

As farmers began moving into this region, the Ohio Company requested Congress to provide some form of government for these people. In 1787 Congress complied by passing another Northwest Ordinance (which became the basis for the political organization of all western lands). By the terms of this ordinance there were to be no slaves in the region north of the Ohio River. The land was to be divided into not less than three nor more than five states. A governor and three judges appointed by Congress (later by the President) sould govern the area until five thousand free male inhabitants had settled there; then these settlers would be allowed to elect a legislative body and to send a non-voting member to Congress. When a proposed state had sixty thousand inhabitants, it would be admitted to the Union "on an equal footing with the original States in all respects whatever."

By the terms of the Northwest Ordinance of 1787, Congress early dedicated itself to an anti-colonial policy. The western lands of the United States eventually were to be given equal standing with the original states, not held as colonial dependencies to be exploited. Such a progressive measure was almost without precedent in world history. And under the terms of these two ordinances the orderly settlement of Ohio proceeded rapidly. Marietta was established in 1788 as was Cincinnati.

Sad as was the central government's record in foreign

affairs, disorganized as was the financial structure of the
country, and ludicrous as was the efforts of Congress to
legislate for the country, it was economic discontent that
largely led to the formation of a "more perfect Union." The
depression which followed the Revolution, caused by the
inability of the national government to gain trade advantages
with European governments and by the narrow-minded
policies of the individual state governments, hit the debtor
class in America very hard. Creditors pressed for payment of
debts which the small farmers had contracted—and a large
majority of the population consisted of small farmers. These
debtors, unable to sell the produce from their farms, could
not pay. The obvious answer, said these farmers and the
small-scale merchants, was for the states to print more
money. The printing of large amounts of money, these people
thought, would solve the depression by causing inflation.
After all, they reasoned, the national Congress had printed
paper money to pay its bills. What had worked at the national
level should also work at the local level.

In seven states this demand became reality, but in
Virginia, Connecticut, Delaware, and Maryland the
legislatures refused. In those states where the demand was
met, however, the paper currency quickly depreciated in
value, and creditors refused to accept it in payment of debts.
In Rhode Island, for example, paper money declined in value
so rapidly that merchants avoided debtors for fear of
payment. The legislature in that state, under the leadership of
radicals, responded by passing a law making refusal to accept
paper money in payment of debts a crime punishable by fine
and imprisonment without trial by jury. A butcher, John
Weeden, appealed his conviction under this law to the state
supreme court; on September 25, 1786, in *Trevett v. Weeden*, the
state supreme court refused to hear the case on the grounds
that it had no jurisdiction in the case, then went on to declare
the law repugnant to the provisions of the state charter (and
therefore unconstitutional). This action set a precedent for
the process of judicial review of legislative acts as to their
constitutionality.

Elsewhere the debtor class was not content with the laws
or the judicial process. They used more direct action. In New

Shay's Rebellion

Hampshire, for example, the militia was called out in 1786 to disperse a mob of debtors demanding passage of a paper money law. The Massachusetts legislature likewise refused to pass such a law, then adjourned for six months in order to avoid the farmer's demands. Farm foreclosures increased in number to such an extent that in August a rebellion occurred. Led by Daniel Shays, a former army officer and an impoverished farmer from the western part of the state, distressed citizens gathered in county conventions to draft resolutions to the legislature, resolutions that declared they were underrepresented in the state legislature, which was true, and that they were the victims of rich men in Boston, partly true. Conventions soon gave way to armed mobs that prevented civil courts (where foreclosure proceedings were heard) from sitting, and then moved to prevent criminal courts (where rioters were tried) from sitting. From there they moved toward the state supreme court at Springfield and even threatened federal arsenals to secure weapons.

Governor James Bowdoin sent General Benjamin Lincoln and six hundred militiamen to protect the supreme court, but Shays and his followers forced it to adjourn on September 26. Then on January 25, 1787, Shays attacked the arsenal at Springfield, but was beaten off by the militia. Two days later a large army of four thousand arrived, and Shays fled through wintery cold to a refuge in Vermont. Shays' Rebellion deeply shocked conservatives, not only in Massachusetts but also in other states. Washington wrote to James Madison about the rebellion and suggested that the United States was "verging to anarchy." Madison replied that a new government was needed, a thought shared by many responsible members of American society.

The present constitution appropriately had its beginnings in the home of George Washington. On March 28, 1785, a convention of delegates from Virginia and Maryland met there to discuss commercial problems; they decided that perhaps congress needed additional powers and suggested a convention to be held at Annapolis the following year. The Annapolis Convention did meet September 11-14, 1786, with delegates in attendance from New York, Pennsylvania, New Jersey, Delaware, and Virginia. The delegates adopted an invitation written by Alexander Hamilton; this called for all thirteen states to send delegates to a convention to meet in Philadelphia in the spring of 1787 for the purpose of discussing commercial matters and to draw up proposed changes in the Articles of Confederation. The impotent congress, which rarely had a quorum, endorsed this call on February 21, 1787, for the *sole and express purpose of revising the Articles of Confederation.*

Signing the Constitution

Embarrassment Ended

Louis Otto, who headed the French legation in the United States, wrote in 1786, "Although there are no nobles in America, there is a class of men denominated 'gentlemen,' who, by reason of their wealth, their talents, their education, their families, or the offices they hold, aspire to a preeminence which the people refuse to grant them." Otto's statement that these men aspired to preeminence was his estimate of their ambitions, but he was totally correct in writing that there was an upper class of "gentlemen." Within three years of the treaty of 1783 which granted the United States its independence, these gentlemen were convinced that the government under the Articles was not capable of guiding the country.

In 1786 George Washington wrote to John Jay, "We have, probably, had too good an opinion of human nature in forming our confederation." John Jay commented that the citizens of the United States needed to become "one nation in every respect," while Oliver Ellsworth wanted "a government capable of controlling the whole, and bringing its force to a point," thereby replacing the "present anarchical confusion prevailing almost everywhere." And James Madison expressed the thought that "men of reflection," even "the most orthodox republicans," wanted a change because of "the existing embarrassments and mortal diseases of the Confederacy."

Madison's comments were important, for he would be one of the most influential men at the constitutional convention. Born on March 5, 1750, at Port Conway, Virginia, he began school at age twelve, studying the classics, as well as French and Spanish. His tutoring completed, he

James Madison

enrolled at the College of New Jersey (Princeton), excelling in history, government, and debating. Graduating in 1771 after two years of study, he remained at the College of New Jersey an additional year to pursue his interest in Hebrew and ethics. Possibly he was considering the ministry as a career, but, returning to Virginia, he grew melancholy. A frail young man who stood only five feet, four inches, he became convinced that he was destined to die young; gradually he withdrew from society.

Two issues of the day roused him from this lethargy: the fight for religious toleration in Virginia and the growing struggle with England. A devout Anglican, Madison nevertheless firmly believed in freedom of conscience. He was elected to the Committee of Safety for Orange County, after which in 1776 his neighbors elected him to the convention that framed a constitution and declaration of rights for Virginia; it was he who offered the resolution subsequently adopted granting religious freedom in that state. Elected to the assembly, he then was named to the Governor's Council in 1778 and two years later sent to represent Virginia in the Congress. Serving in Congress for three years, he was one of the few delegates in regular attendance; he advocated that the central government should have the power to tax, fought for Virginia's rights to its western lands, and helped arrange the famous "three-fifths compromise" whereby five slaves would count as three free persons. In return for this service the state of Virginia often failed to pay him any salary. After Congress moved to Princeton, New Jersey, he gave up his seat in the organization and returned to his home of Montpelier near Charlottesville, there taking up a study of law.

He was allowed little time for his studies or the pursuit of his other interests, however, for his neighbors elected him to the legislature, where he would serve to 1786; there his ideas were evident in many pieces of legislation: to develop the state's commerce, to allow the free exercise of religion, to keep the currency sound, and to aid the back country (which would become Kentucky). Also, he urged that the national government be granted the right to regulate internal and foreign commerce. Because he was a leader in bringing about the series of conferences that would lead to the constitutional convention, he was elected as one of Virginia's delegates to that gathering in Philadelphia when that body was called in 1787.

Many state leaders were aware of the need to revise the government under the Articles of Confederation. Events had made them painfully aware of the defects of that government: the United States was being slighted in international negotiations because of its weakness; England still retained its posts in the old Northwest Territory; Spain was promoting sedition in the Southwest; economic development internally was stifled because of quarrels between the various states; the national government had so little money that it could not meet its obligations; and some states were on a binge of printing paper currency that had little or no value. Yet the Articles could not be amended except by unanimous consent of all the states, and this seemed unattainable—even in the face of such threats as Shays' Rebellion.

The call for a convention to draft some new form of government grew out of none of those problems. Rather it came from the need for regulations to control commerce on the Potomac. When Lord Baltimore had received his charter from the British king for the colony of Maryland, this charter had stipulated that the southern shore of the Potomac was the boundary of Maryland. Thus planters in Virginia using that river to move their goods to market had to comply with Maryland's laws. As early as 1777 a commission from each of these two states had met to work out mutually satisfactory procedures. Because no agreement had been reached, new commissioners were appointed in 1784 and 1785. Early in 1785, five of these commissioners met at Mount Vernon, the plantation of George Washington and drafted recommendations that proved satisfactory to both states. However, these commissioners recognized that other states, especially Pennsylvania and Delaware, had an interest in navigation in this area, and therefore they issued a call for delegates from all states to meet at Annapolis in September 1786 to consider establishing a code of commercial regulations for all the states; in short, these commissioners wanted to end the interstate rivalries and jealousies that were strangling the growth of commerce and industry.

James Madison quickly came to the fore at the meeting—although only five states sent delegates to it. Always dressed in black, he turned his analytical mind to the problems facing the republic. He well knew that the ideals of the revolution were in danger of being lost if the United States was allowed to fragment into thirteen tiny, warring republics. In public a shy, retiring, small man, yet in private a witty—even hilarious—conversationalist, Madison was content at this gathering to allow Alexander Hamilton of New York to play the leading role, while he carefully drafted political essays which he allowed his associates to read.

Alexander Hamilton, who also was small of stature and slight of build, was altogether a different type of individual. Born in 1757 in the Leeward Islands at the British colony of Nevis, his father was Scotch and his mother French Huguenot. Because his father was poor, Hamilton at age twelve began working in a general store; however, because of his obvious brilliance, some of his relatives provided the money for his education. Arriving in New York in 1772, he went to a grammar school for a year, then entered King's College (now Columbia University). His education was interrupted by the Revolution. A staunch patriot as early as 1774, he wrote pamphlets which, although he was only seventeen, showed a remarkable grasp of the issues and a great mind. Commissioned an officer of artillery in 1776, he came to the attention of General George Washington and on March 1, 1777, became secretary and aide-de-camp to that great man. His duties were arduous, for he handled correspondence and provided administrative organization for the busy general.

By the end of the war Hamilton was known in the best circles of colonial society, and had married Elizabeth Schuyler of the Schuyler family of New York. Admitted to the bar in that state in 1781, he had a fair complexion and feminine softness about his face, but bore his slight frame with great dignity. Elected to Congress in November of 1782, he showed himself a believer in a strong central government. Retiring from Congress in 1783, he attended the Annapolis Trade

Alexander Hamilton

(painting by John Trumbull)

Convention convinced that this was an opportunity to strengthen the national government. When he saw that this convention would fail, it was he who drafted the report—which was unanimously accepted—recommending that each state appoint commissioners to meet in Philadelphia in May 1787 "to take into consideration the situation of the United States, to devise such further provisions as shall seem to them necessary to render the Constitution of the Federal Government adequate to the exigencies of the Union, and to report an act for that purpose to the United States in Congress assembled." Later Hamilton maneuvered a motion through both houses of the legislature in New York instructing the state's delegates in the Continental Congress to support a constitutional convention. And he was named one of the three delegates from New York to the convention.

At first it seemed the Continental Congress would allow the call for a convention to die, but several states, such as New York, began naming delegates. Thereupon the Congress, reversing itself, endorsed the convention in February 1787; the convention was to meet *for the sole and express purpose of revising the Articles of Confederation.*" By the following May, when the convention met, only New Hampshire and Rhode Island had failed to appoint deputies. Later New Hampshire would send a delegation—which arrived in time to participate in some of the proceedings. Only Rhode Island stood aloof, although some leading citizens in that state did send letters to the convention pledging their support.

The fifty-five men who at one time or another participated in the debates were among the most distinguished in America. They averaged forty-two years of age, thirty-one had college educations, and half were lawyers. Easily the most outstanding man there, in terms of veneration and awe, was George Washington, and he was chosen to preside over the assembly. Other leading figures included James Madison who would contribute so much that in latter years he would be called the "Father of the Constitution"; William Paterson of New Jersey, who championed the interests of the small states; Alexander Hamilton of New York, who worked for a government with a strong chief executive, but who was absent from many of the deliberations because of the press of his legal work at home; Gouverneur Morris of Pennsylvania, who aided in forming the language of the Constitution; and Benjamin Franklin of Pennsylvania, who effected some of the important compromises there. Other prominent members of the convention included James Wilson of Pennsylvania, Roger Sherman and Oliver Ellsworth of Connecticut, Rufus King and Elbridge Gerry of Massachusetts, John Dickinson of Delaware, Luther Martin of Maryland, and Charles Pinckney, Charles Cotesworth Pinckney, and John Rutledge of South Carolina. The two best-known Americans absent from this meeting were John Adams and Thomas Jefferson. Both were abroad on diplomatic missions for the United States.

As these men gathered, they were aware of the significance of the work they were doing. James Madison believed they would "decide forever the fate of Republican government," while Gouverneur Morris asserted, "The whole human race will be affected by the proceedings of this Convention." James Wilson stated, "After the lapse of six thousand years since the creation of the world America now presents the first instance of a people assembled to weigh deliberately and calmly and to decide leisurely and peaceably upon the form of government by which they will bind themselves and their posterity." Jefferson summed up popular opinion of these men, at least in later years, when he referred to them as "an assembly of demigods."

The meetings were held in an upper room of the State House in Philadelphia. Gathering there on May 25, the delegates quickly were confronted with two alternatives. The first was that the delegates should comply with their instructions and simply prepare amendments to the Articles for submission to all thirteen states for adoption or rejection. The second was that the Articles should be discarded entirely and a new plan of government drafted. Only a short amount of discussion and voting was needed for the second argument to prevail. Then, fearing that the news of this decision would cause a sensation, the members voted to hold their sessions thereafter in secret; sentries were placed at all the doors to keep outsiders away, and they had the streets around the

State House covered with loose earth so that the noise of passing traffic would not disturb their deliberations.

Once the philosophical goal of the convention had been determined—to establish a new form of government—the next step was to begin hammering out the details. Many of the delegates had arrived knowing they were going to draft a constitution for the nation, and some had already drafted proposals for consideration. Edmund Randolph of Virginia presented a plan on May 29, just four days after the meeting commenced, which would become known as the Virginia Plan or large-state plan. This proposed a legislative body with two houses, as was the case in the British Parliament, but with the delegates in both houses apportioned on the basis of population of white males; however, both houses were to have real power (during the past decade the upper house in most state legislatures had no real power, and these leaders in Philadelphia had seen the disastrous results of a single legislative house with almost unlimited powers).

In the two weeks of debate that followed the introduction of the Virginia Plan, much of the discussion concerned the method of selecting delegates to this new legislative body. The Virginia Plan stated that the lower house would be elected by popular vote. Alexander Hamilton argued that the members of the upper house should then be appointed only from the upper class, and that each senator should hold this position for life. He felt this would be necessary in order to curb the excesses of the majority, which was composed of the lower classes. Other members of the convention responded that the United States was not a country where social rank should be entrenched in one house of the national legislative body, as it was in England. The Virginia delegates thereupon proposed that the members of the upper house be elected by the lower house.

The Virginia Plan had other features such as: the chief executive would be chosen by the legislature, and state officials would be bound to support the national government and grant it veto power over state laws. It also included a proposal for a "council of revision," composed of the chief executive and members of the judiciary, which could veto acts of congress.

Roger Sherman

Benjamin Franklin

Delegates from the small states were unhappy with this plan. If both houses of the national legislature were chosen on the basis of population, the large states could dominate. Advocates of the Virginia Plan responded that in a proportionate system the people, rather than the states, should be represented.

On June 15 the small states introduced a plan of their own. Presented by William Paterson of New Jersey, this small-state plan, or New Jersey Plan, proposed a continuation of the Articles of Confederation, however, strengthening Congress by giving it the power to tax imports, regulate trade, and tax directly; the acts of Congress and its treaties would be the "supreme law" of the land; Congress would name a plural chief executive and appoint a supreme court; and the executive branch would be responsible for enforcing the laws passed by Congress. The New Jersey Plan clearly would leave the states dominant and the national government small and subservient except in clearly specified areas.

One last plan was advanced. On June 18 Alexander Hamilton introduced his "propositions" for the consideration of the delegates. He proposed that the Congress should consist of two houses, the lower house to be elected by the people and the upper house to be named by electors chosen by the people. Members of this upper house, along with the chief executive, would serve during good behavior—that is, for life unless they committed some breach of good conduct. All state laws would be strictly subordinate to national laws, while the state governors would be named by the chief executive. Under this plan the central government clearly would be superior to the state governments.

As the debate continued through the hot, muggy days of June, the delegates had several alternatives before them. The basic dilemma was the question of what type of government the nation was to have: a weak central government and strong states, or a strong central government and weak states. The ideal of local self-government was attractive to all of them, yet they knew from their immediate past experience of rebellions, of cheap paper money, and of trade restrictions between the states that the national government had to have real powers if the nation was to survive and be respectable in the international community. These discussions of the last two weeks of June were conducted with good humor, with respect, and with decorum. Obviously one side would win and the other lose; the question was which.

On June 29 a vote was taken of the state delegations (each state having one vote) on the issue of the makeup of the lower house of the national legislature. In this the majority voted for proportional representation in the lower house. This house it was agreed should be the point of origin for all money bills. But on the issue of representation in the upper house, the vote on July 2 was a tie. A committee was chosen to consider this matter, each state having one member on the committee; the members of this committee were chosen by ballot—and the small states obviously won. However, what the committee decided had to receive the approval of the entire convention. Obviously a compromise would have to be arranged.

The issue was debated for two more weeks. Then the weather suddenly turned cool, and with this tempers lessened. On July 16 a proposal was made by Roger Sherman of Connecticut, afterwards called the Connecticut Compromise or the Great Compromise. This provided for a lower house of Congress elected on the basis of population and an upper house elected on the basis of two per state. In determining representation in the lower house, five slaves were to count as three free men, while the members of the upper house were to be elected by the legislatures in the states. This would insure a balance of powers between the larger states and the small ones. In short, the Great Compromise provided for "federalism"—a division of powers whereby the national government was to have specified power, while local matters were to be left to local governments.

Delegates from the large states were deeply disappointed at this compromise and at first decided to call for an adjournment to allow time for the delegates from those states to consider what they should do. However, they refrained for fear they would be accused of breaking up the convention. The members from the small states, thereafter proved much more willing to compromise. All realized that there were too many delegates anxious to debate every step to proceed

rapidly, so in order to hasten their work, the convention
voted to create a committee of five members whose task it
would be to draft a constitution setting up the machinery of
government. The members of this committee, created on July
26, were John Rutledge, Edmund Randolph, Nathaniel
Gorham, Oliver Ellsworth, and James Wilson. Congress then
adjourned for ten days.

The members of this drafting committee apparently
worked almost night and day including Sunday to complete
their task in just ten days. Drawing upon state constitutions,
the British system of government, the Virginia and New
Jersey plans, and the details already agreed upon by the
convention, they completed a document closely resembling
the modern Constitution—although many parts were in
different order than they would be in the finished product.
Their work, presented to the other members when the
convention resumed its deliberations on August 6, was
printed on seven folio pages—each of which had a wide
margin for notes and suggested changes.

For the next five weeks the delegates discussed, added to,
subtracted from, and reworked each sentence. At first their
major concern was the Congress of the new government;
approximately sixty percent of the finished document would
deal with Congress, its powers, and its limitations. Congress
was given the power to tax directly, to declare war and
suppress insurrections, to regulate commerce, to coin money,
and to make treaties binding on the states. Moreover, it could
make "all laws which shall be necessary and proper for
carrying into execution the foregoing," as well as all laws
necessary for the "general welfare of the United States."
These clauses were inserted to make certain that the new
government would never be as restricted—and impotent—as
had the government under the Articles of Confederation.
However, the framers of the Constitution did not want
Congress to be all-powerful and therefore placed restrictions
on it. The chief executive was given the power to veto its
acts, but this veto could be overridden by a two-thirds vote of
both houses. The framers placed a limitation on the power of
Congress by spelling out exactly what constituted treason:
some overt act to which two witnesses testified in open court;

Congress might define the punishment for treason, but the deed itself was clearly delineated in the Constitution.

During this haggling about the powers of Congress, members from Northern states wanted to give the new legislative body the power to pass navigation acts that would require American products to be carried in American ships. Southerners, who exported their farm produce and imported manufactured goods, wanted their products to move the cheapest possible way. On the other hand, Southerners wanted no restrictions on the importation of slaves, which some Northerners opposed. The result again was compromise. Southerners did agree to a provision that Congress could pass restrictive legislation related to shipping by a simple majority, while Northerners agreed that Congress would not interfere with the importation of slaves for twenty years. As to slavery itself, the Constitution was mute. As Oliver Ellsworth stated, "The morality or wisdom of slavery are considerations belonging to the States themselves."

These founding fathers tried to remedy one other defect of the government under the Articles: the lack of a chief executive. Almost unanimously they agreed that there should be a separate executive branch of government, headed by a single man—the President. Obviously modeled after the governorship of individual states, the President was to serve for four years, not for life as Hamilton had advocated and not for a single year as others had wished, but he could be reelected. The President would be elected, not directly by the people and not by the state legislatures, but by an electoral college selected by the voters. The framers of the Constitution did not trust the people sufficiently to trust them with electing a President. Each state's electorate could select as many members of the electoral college as it had Congressmen, which was another compromise between the large and the small states. In the electoral college the members were to vote for two men, one of whom was not from their own state. The person receiving the most votes in the electoral college would become the President, and the person receiving the second highest total would become the Vice-President.

The members of the constitutional convention believed

that only in one election out of an approximate twenty would one candidate receive a majority of the votes in the electoral college and thereby become the President. Further they believed that in nineteen out of twenty elections no person would get a majority, and the election thereby would be thrown into the House of Representatives where each state would have one vote. This procedure would allow the large states, with their larger Congressional delegations and thus greater vote in the electoral college, to select the presidential candidates, while the smaller states would choose from among the top three candidates to name the President in the House of Representatives.

The President would have the power to appoint his administrative staff, along with ambassadors and other high officials, but he was restrained by the necessity of securing Senatorial consent to these appointments. Moreover, he was given the function of conducting foreign affairs—subject to the "advise and consent" of the Senate. The President, in addition, was to be commander-in-chief of the army and navy, and he had the power to veto acts of Congress—subject to their passage over his veto by a two-thirds vote in both houses.

As to the third branch of the national government, the judiciary, the Constitution contained surprisingly little. It did provide that the chief court of the land would be the Supreme Court of the United States; this court could hear cases on appeal from the lower courts, as Congress established them, and from state courts in cases involving the Constitution, cases involving treaties with foreign powers, and cases involving foreigners and lawsuits between states and citizens of different states. In the Constitution there was no specific mention of the process of judicial review (that is, review by the courts of acts of Congress for their constitutionality). However, the principle is implied, for the Constitution does specify that state laws contrary to the national Constitution and to federal law must give way—and only the courts can determine which state laws are contrary to federal laws and the Constitution. To protect the members of the judiciary from political influence, the Constitution stipulates that they serve indefinitely on good behavior. The only way they can be removed is by impeachment, death, or voluntary retirement.

By the end of August the members of the constitutional convention clearly were growing tired and restive. For more than three months they had been working with, as one member confided to his diary, just five cool days. Those members who wanted to tarry overlong to argue some minute point found themselves voted down in short order. Finally on September 8 a new committee was appointed, one of five members to "revise the stile of and arrange the articles which had been agreed to by the House." Chosen by ballot, this committee consisted of Dr. W.S. Johnson, Alexander Hamilton, Gouverneur Morris, James Madison, and Rufus King. Four days later the committee had completed its work; publicly most of the credit for the improvements in style were given to Morris, for he was widely regarded as a man of great powers of expression. The document then was printed again, and on Thursday, the thirteenth, the delegates began a three-day close, line-by-line reading, some final changes being inserted. On Saturday, September 15, the delegates ordered that the Constitution be printed in final form.

The final meeting of the constitutional convention was on Monday, September 17. Some of those attending that day were unwilling to sign the document that had been drafted, yet the majority wished their work to appear to be unanimously accepted. Gouverneur Morris thereupon suggested a way out to please both sides; at his urging the final sentence of the new Constitution read, "Done in Convention by the unanimous consent of the states present... in witness whereof we have hereunto subscribed our names." This gave the appearance that the work was satisfactory to all delegates, but only thirty-nine of them, representing twelve states, signed it.

The document they had produced, one with which every member of the convention could find something wrong, was a curious blend of past colonial history, of the British heritage of Parliamentary government, of political theory traceable to a dozen and more thinkers, of some of the experiments in the various states during the Revolution, and of pure innovation. They had tried to separate and balance the powers of government between three distinct branches: the judiciary, the executive, and the legislative—all within a federal framework that allowed most powers to reside in the individual state and local governments. And it was an eminently practical—rather than theoretical—government that they conceived; there were no great flights of beautiful rhetoric in the Constitution, as would be contained in the French constitution written during their revolution two years later. The framers of the American Constitution were practical men of affairs, who drafted a document that would work.

The most revolutionary concept in the Constitution was not in the legislative or the judicial or even the executive branches of this new government. Rather the real revolution was in its decision about the origin of sovereignty. During the Revolution the colonists had argued with British thinkers about which was sovereign: the king, Parliament, or the colonial legislatures. The framers of the Constitution boldly asserted that none of these was the source of legitimacy for government, for governments were instituted by people and legitimately had only those powers which the people delegated to them. Thus they began their document, "We the people of the United States...." And from this concept came yet another revolutionary approach—the method of ratification.

When the delegates concluded their work, they decided that their handiwork should be ratified not by Congress or even by the state legislatures, but rather by the people themselves through elected representative assemblies. The people in each state were asked to elect special constitutional ratification assemblies to pass on the document. Another revolutionary feature of this Constitution was that it was to become operative when adopted by only nine of the thirteen states; under the Articles of Confederation the approval of all thirteen states had been necessary for any change in the basic organ of government, but the Articles were to be overturned by roughly a two-thirds vote of the people of the various states.

As the constitutional convention adjourned, a woman hurried up to Benjamin Franklin and asked, "Well, Doctor, what have we got? A republic or a monarchy?"

Franklin responded, "A republic—if you can keep it!"

Before the republic could be preserved, however, the Constitution had to be adopted—and opposition began the same day that George Washington signed the document as president of the convention and a delegate from Virginia. Anti-Federalists, as they were called, quickly began to denounce the Constitution as an instrument which would take sovereignty away from the states and place it in the hands of national officials. Debtors were against a national government with the power to tax and regulate currency; such a system would militate against them, for it would force them to repay their debts with hard currency. Finally, there were citizens concerned that a national government might destroy individual liberty. Some of these Anti-Federalists possessed little wealth, some were young, some were intellectuals; however, some were wealthy, some were elderly, some unschooled. Division over acceptance or rejection of this Constitution was not along class, economic, social or even intellectual lines.

In some states the Federalists, as those favoring the Constitution came to be known, moved so quickly that opposition could not be organized. In Pennsylvania—with enthusiasm for the Constitution running high in Philadelphia—a motion was introduced in the Pennsylvania Assembly to call a ratifying convention. When that body convened, the Anti-Federalist members tried to prevent a vote by removing themselves from the Assembly so that no quorum could be established. Indignant citizens went to the homes of two of the legislators, dragged them to the State House, and forcibly held them in their seats until a quorum could be established. The Assembly then voted to call a ratifying convention, an act that brought forth wild celebrations in the City of Brotherly Love. In the elections that followed to choose delegates, the Federalists clearly dominated. When this gathering convened near the end of November, the Anti-Federalists tried to delay the proceedings by arguing endlessly over every word, but on December 12 by a vote of forty-six to twenty-three they ratified the Constitution.

Pennsylvania was not the first to ratify the document,

however. While the delegates in Pennsylvania had quibbled
about words, a convention met in Delaware and on December
7 unanimously voted acceptance. In New Jersey the delegates
chosen spent only a week debating and on December 18 voted
almost unanimously for the Constitution. In Georgia, where
the local citizens wanted national help in conquering the
Creek Indians, the Constitution was unanimously accepted on
January 2, 1788. In Connecticut the ratifying convention met
only five days before ratifying the document by a margin of
three to one. Thus far the Federalists could be extremely
pleased, for they had encountered little real opposition; but
with the exception of Pennsylvania those states that had
ratified the document were either small or of little national
importance. The states that really mattered were Virginia,
New York, and Massachusetts; without any one of these, the
new nation would have little chance of success.

When the delegates met in Massachusetts, on the same
day that the delegates in Connecticut adjourned, the first
note of discontent was sounded. The members elected in
Boston, like those of Philadelphia, were strongly Federalist in
sentiment, but those from the back country—where Shays
had his strength—were opposed to any reduction in state
power. Even those Federalists among the 355 delegates in
Massachusetts were unhappy that the new Constitution
contained no Bill of Rights guaranteeing individual liberties.
Both Federalists and Anti-Federalists assessed the vote as
roughly even, neither side having a majority. Two members,
Governor John Hancock and Samuel Adams, seemed to hold
the key to which way the vote would go. Both finally agreed
to accept the new document, believing that it would be easier
to add a Bill of Rights to the Constitution than it would be to
call a new constitutional convention. In the end the vote on
February 6 was 187 for and 168 against, but with an urgent
recommendation that amendments be added to guarantee
individual liberties. In fact, the ratification convention in
Massachusetts drafted nine such amendments and urged that
future Congressmen from the state should "exert all their
influence, and use all reasonable and legal methods, To obtain
a ratification of the said alterations and provisions."

Thomas Jefferson, who was in Paris representing the

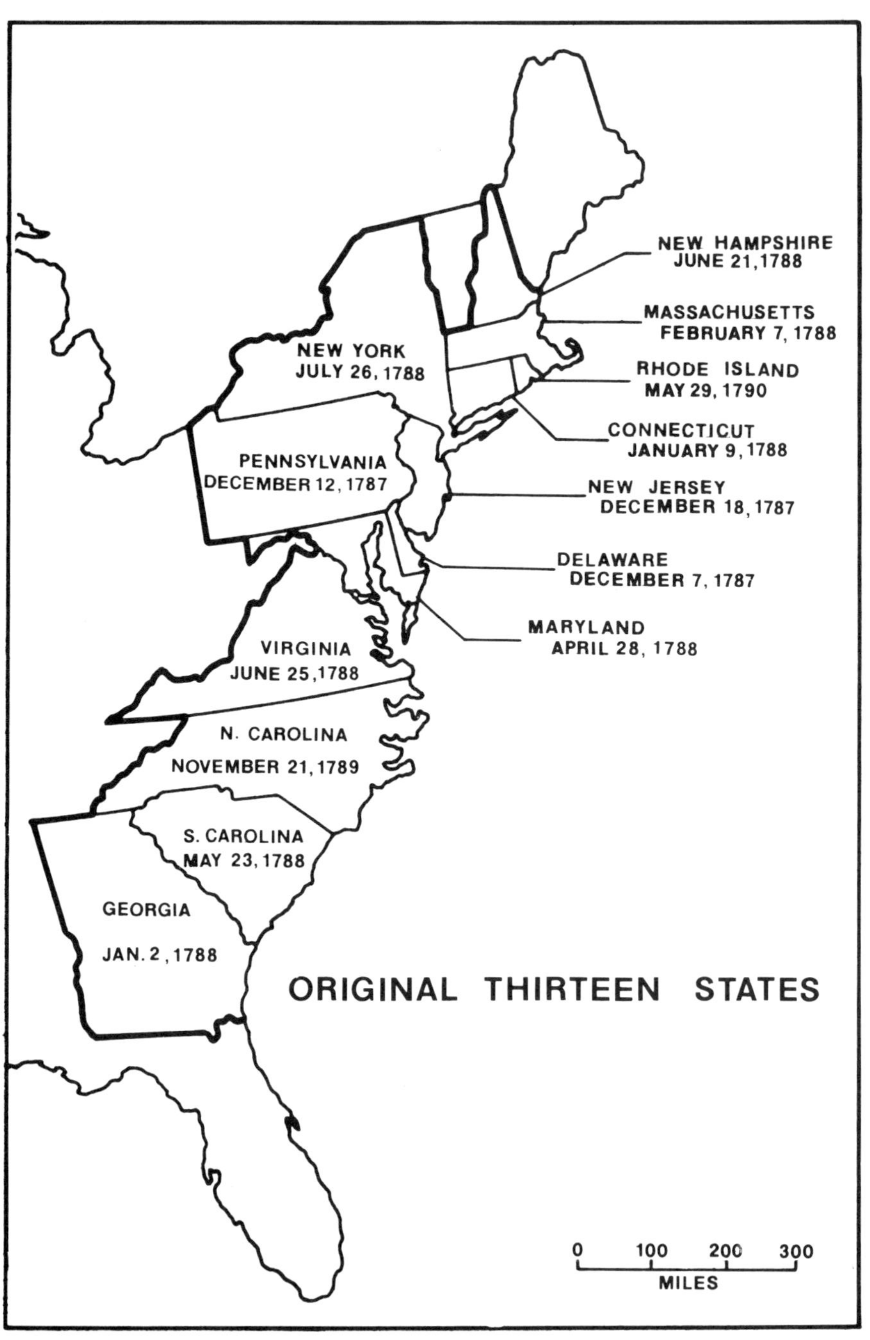

NEW HAMPSHIRE
JUNE 21, 1788
MASSACHUSETTS
FEBRUARY 7, 1788
RHODE ISLAND
MAY 29, 1790
CONNECTICUT
JANUARY 9, 1788
NEW JERSEY
DECEMBER 18, 1787
DELAWARE
DECEMBER 7, 1787
MARYLAND
APRIL 28, 1788
NEW YORK
JULY 26, 1788
PENNSYLVANIA
DECEMBER 12, 1787
VIRGINIA
JUNE 25, 1788
N. CAROLINA
NOVEMBER 21, 1789
S. CAROLINA
MAY 23, 1788
GEORGIA
JAN. 2, 1788
ORIGINAL THIRTEEN STATES
0   100   200   300
MILES

United States, agreed with the Massachusetts delegates. To Madison he wrote, "I wish with all my soul that the nine first conventions may accept the new Constitution, to secure to us the good it contains; but I equally wish that the four latest, whichever they may be, may refuse to accede to it till a declaration of rights be annexed."

Maryland, where the vote came next, was easily under Federalist control, and the vote there on April 26 was sixty-three to eleven in favor of the Constitution. Likewise, South Carolina favored the document on May 28 by a strong majority. The ninth state to ratify was New Hampshire, which did so on June 21 by a vote of fifty-seven to forty-seven. Technically the Constitution thereupon became effective—although a convention in one state had rejected it. In Rhode Island, where the debtor class was strongly in control, the vote there on March 24—by referendum—was negative.

Even with nine states ratifying the Constitution, leading Federalists knew that a union of the states would be futile without New York and Virginia, and in both there were powerful men opposing adoption of the new organ of government. George Washington and James Madison openly urged adoption, but Patrick Henry, George Mason, and Richard Henry Lee were vocal in denouncing the document. As in Massachusetts the major criticism of the Constitution was that it carried no guarantees of individual liberties—no Bill of Rights. The Federalists responded that these could be added quickly by amendment, but when the ratifying convention finally met in June 1788 the issue was still much in doubt. After four days of debate, however, the delegates on June 25 ratified the Constitution by a vote of eighty-nine to seventy-nine "with a hope of obtaining amendments" that would keep the national government from becoming tyrannical.

Just eight days previous to Virginia's ratification, the convention for New York met, and those knowledgeable observers who predicted the outcome estimated that two-thirds of the delegates opposed acceptance of the Constitution. However, the positive vote in Virginia, coming soon after the opening of the convention in New York, disorganized the Anti-Federalists there. Principally the credit for the outcome in New York went to Alexander Hamilton who, although unhappy that the projected national government would not be stronger, nonetheless wanted it adopted. Knowing that the outcome in New York rested with the educated segment of the population, he determined that a series of essays should be published in the newspapers; these would explain the new form of government, answer the critics of it, and show the philosophical concepts embodied in it. With the assistance of James Madison and John Jay, he saw to the publication of eighty-five essays under the name "Publius." Hamilton wrote approximately fifty of these, Madison thirty, and Jay five. Later these would collectively be known as *The Federalist Papers*. Some of these were written to counteract a host of articles and pamphlets written in opposition to the Constitution, most of them anonymously under such names as Cato, Brutus, and even Caesar.

Published between October 1787 and May 1788, these essays form the most important discussion of the concept of federalism ever written. Madison, for example, wrote in one of his essays the startling idea that a republican form of government would work better in a large country than in a small one, an idea in direct opposition to the statement of William Lenoir of North Carolina that "no extensive empire can be governed upon republican principles" and that "such a government will degenerate into a despotism." Madison responded that in a small nation a small economic oligarchy could easily secure a lasting ascendancy to trample on the rights of the majority. In a large nation, he said, various economic interests would balance one another just as there would be balance through sectional rivalries; therefore tyranny would be impossible to establish. And, argued the authors of *The Federalist Papers*, the rights of the minority would be protected from the vicious attacks of the majority, while a national government would attract to its service the brightest and best minds for the good of all.

This strong exposition and explanation of the Constitution had the desired effect. The tide did turn in New York, and the vote, taken on July 26, favored ratification by the narrow margin of thirty to twenty-seven. The future of the United States was assured, for all the big states had accepted it. Almost everywhere in the nation there was rejoicing, especially on that July 4, 1788.

Yet this enthusiasm was tempered by the knowledge that North Carolina and Rhode Island had as yet not accepted the Constitution. When the ratification convention met in North Carolina on July 21, it was overwhelmingly Anti-Federalist in sentiment. However, news of ratification in New York tempered the delegates to postpone final action; by a vote of 185 to 84 they decided to adjourn without reaching a decision. Thus neither North Carolina nor Rhode Island, which earlier had rejected the Constitution, were part of the Union when the federal government went into operation. Only after Congress threatened the two recalcitrant states with economic duties and treatment as foreign nations did they consent to join. North Carolina finally ratified the compact on November 21, 1789, after the Bill of Rights had been proposed in Congress, and Rhode Island surrendered on May 29, 1790, by the narrow margin of only two votes after Congress seemed in a mood forcibly to collect that state's share of the cost of the Revolution.

The new Union had been forged—but the government created on paper had to be transferred into the realm of reality. The visionary schemes of the founding fathers had to be put into operation. The Congress of the Articles of Confederation, still in operation during this time of ratification, agreed with the will of the people, and voted itself into oblivion. On September 13 it voted that New York City would be the site of the new government and established March 4, 1789, as the date for the first meeting of the new Congress. Before adjourning on October 10, 1788, the Congress of the Confederation determined that presidential electors were to be chosen on the first Wednesday in January and cast their ballots on the first Wednesday in February. Thereafter the United States would be governed under the Constitution forged at Philadelphia between May and September of 1787.

That document in itself constituted a new American Revolution, for it overthrew the old government and instituted another one. The document, drawn from the thoughts of European philosophers such as John Locke,

Voltaire, Montesquieu, and David Hume, embodied the
principle that legitimate authority for government comes
from below—from the people—not from above, that men
have natural rights, that the powers of government should be
balanced and checked, that all men should stand equal before
the law, and that most power should be retained at the state
or local level. These ideas were revolutionary, but equally
revolutionary was the method by which they were adopted.
The delegates to the constitutional convention had met with
specific instructions to revise the Articles of Confederation;
instead they had drawn up a document abolishing that old
government and substituting a new one. Some historians
have labeled the Constitution and the federal government
instituted under it *"The Revolution of 1789."* So it was: a
peaceful revolution, a welcome revolution, a revolution
without bloodshed—but a revolution nonetheless in that 200
years of colonial experience had been embodied in a written
document.

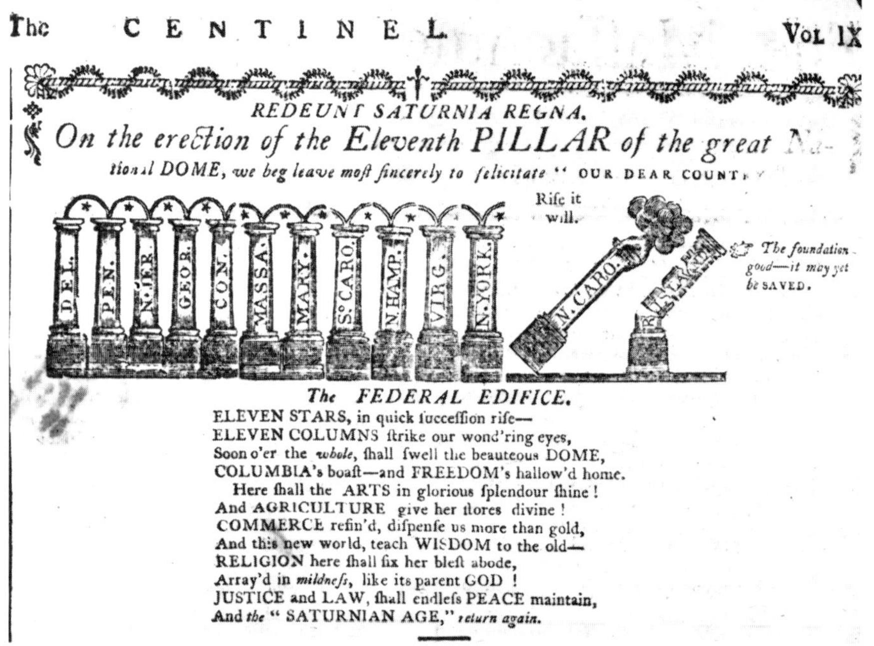

A cartoon appearing at the time of the beginning of the government under the Constitution

Completing the Task 6

Alexander Hamilton, in Number 84 of *The Federalist Papers*, attempted to answer criticisms in New York—and elsewhere—that the Constitution needed a Bill of Rights appended in order to insure individual liberties and to protect the people from tyrannical government. *"The Constitution is itself, in every rational sense, and to every useful purpose, A BILL OF RIGHTS,"* he asserted, for he felt that additional words would not guarantee the rights of the people any more than already contained in the basic document. Because the Constitution stated, "We, the people of the United States," he contended no government ever could consider itself superior to those who ordained and established the Constitution—and in his writing he italicized *ordain* and *establish*. In fact, he boldly stated "that bills of rights, in the sense and to the extent in which they are contended for, are not only unnecessary in the proposed Constitution, but would even be dangerous," for these "would contain various exceptions to powers not granted; and, on this very account, would afford a colorable pretext to claim more than were granted."

Despite Hamilton's reasoned and cogent arguments, the ratification convention in New York, after voting in favor of the Constitution, strongly urged "their Representatives in the Congress, to Exert all their Influence, and use all reasonable means to Obtain a Ratification" of no less than thirty-two proposed amendments.

New York's delegates to a ratification convention were not alone in their demand for a Bill of Rights. In

Massachusetts the delegates had expressed fears about what they called "undue administration of the Federal Government." By this, specifically, they meant the power of the national government to tax the people directly; however, three of the amendments they wished attached to the Constitution dealt with civil rights. Maryland's delegates accepted the Constitution without reservations, but there was considerable debate about the need for amendments. In South Carolina the delegates wanted to limit the power of Congress in the field of taxation, while in New Hampshire the delegates suggested the same list of amendments as in Massachusetts. And in Virginia opponents of the Constitution fought it on the basis that it did not contain a Bill of Rights; in the end these delegates accepted the argument of James Madison and his friends that the document should be ratified as it was and then work for amendments, particularly those guaranteeing free speech, a free press, and freedom of religion.

The Congress of the Articles of Confederation, shortly before it adjourned, called for the new Congress under the Constitution to meet in New York City on March 4, 1789, which it subsequently did. George Washington, as President, noted in his first message to that body the widespread demand for amendments, but he declined to make any "particular recommendations on this subject." For the next two months, however, Congress was too occupied with other matters, particularly with establishing the machinery of government, to take up the question.

James Madison, who had been elected to that new Congress, finally took the initiative to keep the promise he had made in Virginia. On May 4, during debate on taxes on imports, he announced his intention to bring up the matter of "amendments to the constitution" on May 25. The timing of his announcement may have been caused by his knowledge that the following day another Congressman from Virginia was going to introduce a measure passed by the legislature of his home state calling for a second constitutional convention, one which would draft a Bill of Rights. Moreover, just two days later a similar call would be introduced from New York. Apparently Madison's statement of his intentions satisfied those Congressmen wishing to amend the Constitution, for no convention was authorized.

May 25 came and went without Madison proposing amendments. Apparently the debate over import duties was still raging too heavily, for he waited two additional weeks. Then on June 8 he spoke at the beginning of the session, saying that he intended to introduce amendments "and advocate them until they should be finally adopted or rejected...." There was immediate opposition; one Congressman from Georgia suggested that tax measures were more important than constitutional amendments, for "without revenue the wheels of Government cannot move." Madison responded that Congress should delay no longer in passing amendments guaranteeing basic rights; additional delays would occasion public suspicion, for the people "may not think we are sincere in our desire to incorporate such amendments in the constitution as will secure those rights, which they consider as not sufficiently guarded."

When other Congressmen continued to oppose Madison, he arose and delivered a speech about his proposed amendments and why he considered them necessary:

> The applications for amendments come from a very respectable number of our constituents, and it is certainly proper for Congress to consider the subject, in order to quiet that anxiety which prevails in the public mind. Indeed, I think it would have been of advantage to the Government, if it had been practicable to have made some proposition for amendments the first business we entered upon; it would have stifled the voice of complaint, and made friends of many who doubted the merits of the constitution. Our future measures would then have been more generally agreeably supported; but the justifiable anxiety to put the Government into operation prevented that; it therefore remains for us to take it up as soon as possible. I wish then to commence the consideration at the present moment; I hold it to be my duty to unfold my ideas, and explain myself to the House in some form or other without delay.

When some opponents argued that all necessary guarantees of individual rights already were contained in the

Constitution, Madison replied that Congress therefore had nothing to lose and everything to gain by inserting amendments to that effect. "The great mass of the people" who opposed the Constitution, he reminded his audience, did so "because it did not contain effectual provisions against encroachments on particular rights." Thus, by adding a Bill of Rights, even if one was unnecessary, the Congress thereby would gain greater popular support for the government.

One of Madison's colleagues from Virginia, Alexander White, saw the need for a Bill of Rights in even stronger terms than Madison: "I venture to affirm, that unless you take early notice of this subject, you will not have power to deliberate. The people will clamor for a new convention; they will not trust the House any longer."

Madison then moved that a select committee be appointed to consider and report amendments—and to it he recommended those amendments "which have occurred to me" as proper for Congress to recommend to the state legislatures. His list consisted of eight potential amendments, one of them having nine separate guarantees. His first was a clear statement that "all power is originally rested in, and consequently derived from, the people," and that the people could change that form of government when they so desired. His second and third amendments dealt with the size of the House of Representatives, providing that no changes in the pay of Congressmen would go into effect until after the next election. And the last five amendments he proposed contained essentially the guarantees that would become the Bill of Rights itself.

Madison intended that his amendments would be inserted directly into the body of the Constitution rather than be appended thereto as numbered amendments. However, Roger Sherman of Connecticut made the motion that these be added after the original document rather than inserted into it. And he spoke in favor of the necessity of a Bill of Rights: "I do not suppose the constitution to be perfect.... I do not expect any perfection on this side of the grave in the works of man...." After some argument in the House about the need for such amendments, Madison spoke again—and made what would become the classic statement on

the need for a Bill of Rights, arguing that if such rights were
inserted in the Constitution, then the courts would be
obligated to enforce them: "independent tribunals of justice
will consider themselves in a peculiar manner the guardians
of those rights."

The final result of the debate on June 8 was to refer
Madison's proposals to the House, which was to act as a
Committee of the Whole. There followed a period of six
weeks in which other matters were considered. Finally on July
21 Madison arose in the House again to propose that the body
go into a Committee of the Whole to consider his
amendments. The same arguments for and against
amendments followed, at the end of which the House voted
thirty-four to fifteen to refer the matter to a committee
consisting of one member from each state. Madison was
appointed to this eleven-member committee (Rhode Island
and North Carolina had not yet ratified the Constitution, and
thus had no Congressional delegation); the only other
member of any distinction was Roger Sherman.

This small committee did its work rapidly. One week
later, on July 28, John Vining of Delaware, the chairman,
reported their labors to the full House. They had rewritten
Madison's proposed amendments, making no substantial
alterations other than stylistic ones. This report laid on the
table of the House until August 3 when Madison again
reminded his colleagues of the need for action. He moved—
and the House agreed—that on August 12 the body would go
into a Committee of the Whole to debate the matter.
However, on the day appointed the members were busy with
other issues and postponed action until the next day. The
House then sat as a Committee of the Whole until August 18
and then for six more days as the House itself, all the while
debating the need for amendments, drafting the proposed
amendments, and determining their fate.

That some members of the House thought a Bill of
Rights to be a small issue can be inferred from the immediate
debate on August 13. Several members argued that the
House had before it several matters "of more importance."
Madison responded, "Is it desireable to keep up a division
among the people of the United States on a point in which

they consider their most essential rights are concerned?" In short, he thought his amendments should be passed in order to lessen opposition to the Constitution.

The first amendment occasioned heated debate, some members arguing that passage of a guarantee of religious freedom might "have a tendency to abolish religion altogether"—meaning that some Americans might consider religious freedom to mean the right of religious license. Madison responded that the amendment was needed to prevent Congress from passing any law infringing upon "the rights of conscience" or from establishing a national church. In this same amendment were guarantees of freedom of speech, press, assembly, and petition. Once past this thorny matter, the House moved faster, the temper of the members matching that of the weather—which was warm.

On August 17 came the second amendment—the right of the people to keep and bear arms. A prohibition against the quartering of soldiers—the third amendment—passed with little debate; the memory of this practice by the British during the colonial period was still fresh. Similarly the fourth amendment, this one guaranteeing the people the right to "be secure in their persons, houses, papers, and effects, against unreasonable searches and seizures" sailed through; again, all members of the House remembered only too well the British practice of using writs of assistance as general search warrants.

Debate over the items covered in what would become the fifth amendment took longer. In British common law it was well established that a witness could not be compelled to testify against himself, as was the concept of double jeopardy (trying a person twice for the same offense). Perhaps most important, however, was the defeat of a motion by George Partridge of Massachusetts to limit double jeopardy only in national cases. Had this motion carried, a person could have been tried twice for the same crime, once in the federal courts and again in a state court. Amendments six and seven, concerning an accused person's right to trial by jury and the assistance of legal counsel, and the right of persons in civil suits to request trial by jury, were readily agreed to by the members. The eighth amendment caused considerably more debate—one which still continues. Some argued that the phrases, "excessive bail" and "excessive fines," were vague, but the statement that "cruel and unusual punishments" should not be inflicted caused Samuel Livermore to complain that "villains often deserve whipping, and perhaps having their ears cut off; but are we in the future to be prevented from inflicting these punishments because they are cruel?"

These first eight amendments were specifically aimed at preserving individual liberties and rights, while the last two concerned reserved powers. The ninth stated, "The enumeration in the Constitution, of certain rights, shall not be construed to deny or disparage others retained by the people," while the tenth stated, "The powers not delegated to the United States by the Constitution, nor prohibited by it to the States, are reserved to the States respectively, or to the people." Some members of the House wanted to make these clauses even more restrictive; Thomas Tucker of South Carolina, for example, wished to insert the word "expressly" into the tenth amendment so that it would read, "The powers not *expressly* delegated to the United States . . . are reserved to the States respectively, or to the people." Madison was moved to exclaim, "It is impossible to confine a Government to the exercise of express powers; there must necessarily be admitted powers by implication, unless the Constitution descended to recount every minutia."

By the close of business on August 18, the House, sitting as a Committee of the Whole, had completed its consideration of the amendments offered by Madison. The following day, sitting as the House, it again went through the proposed measures. The first measure was a formal vote on a motion by Roger Sherman of Connecticut that the Bill of Rights be appended to the Constitution rather than inserted therein; this carried—and thus Sherman, an opponent of the Bill of Rights, was responsible for setting these measures in a separate place, thereby giving them added significance. Minor corrections were made, while others were rejected, and by August 22 the House was agreeable to what had been accomplished. These then were sent to a three-man committee to be arranged in order.

This report contained seventeen proposed amendments.

Two of these concerned Congress—how representatives were to be selected and the pay of Congressmen—while others later would be combined to make the ten that finally became known as the Bill of Rights. The report was made on August 24 to the House, which passed them and sent them to the Senate.

The amendments passed by the House first were read in the Senate on August 25, at which time an effort was made to postpone Senate action on them until the following session. This was defeated, and debate began on them September 2. A flood of additional proposed amendments were introduced—and rejected—whereupon the Senate proceeded to pare down the House list of seventeen to twelve by combining some. In most cases it just polished the wording into the final form.

The Senate did attempt to weaken the intent of the amendment on freedom of religion. Richard Henry Lee, a devout Anglican, secured the help of zealots of the Congregationalist persuasion to rewrite what eventually became the first amendment to read that Congress would "make no law establishing articles of faith or a mode of worship or prohibiting the free exercise of religion." This would have opened a loophole so that eventually Congress might extend financial support to one denomination or another.

Such changes naturally had to be ironed out in a conference committee between the two houses of Congress. The three members from the House were Madison, Vining, and Sherman—and Madison took the lead in forcing a return to the original intent of his amendment. Madison's knowledge of British history told him that, without freedom of religion and separation of church and state, there never could be true freedom of speech or of the press or of the right of assembly He was able to secure Senate acceptance of an even stronger statement about the separation of church and state: "Congress shall make no law respecting an establishment of religion or prohibiting the free exercise thereof." On September 9 the Senate agreed with a resolution of the House that the new wording was acceptable in all twelve amendments. George Washington officially transmitted them to the states for acceptance or rejection on October 2.

Most states in 1789, and for years thereafter, did not print their proceedings, as was the case with Congress, and thus historians are left with few tangible documents with which to study the process of ratification in the legislatures. Maryland became the first state to complete action on the proposed twelve amendments; early in 1790 it accepted the entire package. Votes in other states came fast in the following months, for the legislature was in session in most states during this time. Rhode Island became the ninth state to accept ten of the twelve amendments when it voted favorably on June 2. However, the vote of ten states was necessary to make them formally a part of the Constitution (for the vote of three-fourths of the states is necessary). Thus the action of the assembly in Virginia became critical.

In that state the House of Delegates accepted the package almost unanimously in December of 1789, but the Senate, Anti-Federalist in its majority, was already disposed to reject anything which came from the nation's capital. Two United States Senators from the state, Richard Henry Lee and William Grayson, wrote denouncing Congress—and especially James Madison—for not including an amendment restricting the power of the national government to tax individuals directly. By a vote of eight to seven the state Senate voted to amend the resolution of the Virginia House of Delegates by striking out several of the popular amendments, stating specifically that the guarantee of religious freedom was not sufficiently strong. Two long years passed before public opinion—and new elections—changed the attitude in the Senate in Virginia, and it voted to accept the amendments.

Not all these amendments then went into force, however. In Delaware, New Hampshire, New Jersey, New York, and Pennsylvania, the legislatures rejected the first two of the amendments proposed by Congress, the two modifying the method of selecting members of Congress and restricting pay raises for Congressmen. This left the remaining ten in the order that they now appear.

Three states did not agree to the amendments at that time. In Massachusetts, according to the *Journals* of its legislature, both houses apparently accepted nine of the twelve amendments. They rejected the first two and the twelfth. However, for some inexplicable reason no official notice to this effect was ever transmitted to the Secretary of State. Thomas Jefferson, who occupied that office, wrote to Christopher Gore, clerk of the legislature, on August 8, 1791, inquiring about the matter. Gore on August 18 responded, "The Senate agreed to all the amendments except the 1st and 2d—the House concurr'd except as to the 12th. The Senate agreed to the alteration of the house, & appointed two of their body, with such as the house should join, to bring in a bill declaratory of their assent—the house joined one of their members to the committee—It does not appear that the Committee ever reported any bill...."

In Connecticut and Georgia the legislatures took no action on the amendments in the belief that no changes in the Constitution were necessary. Without their assent, however, the necessary three-fourths of the states had ratified the ten amendments known as the Bill of Rights, and on March 1, 1792, Thomas Jefferson as Secretary of State sent a letter to the governors of all the states formally and officially notifying them—and sending them copies—"of certain articles in addition and amendment of the Constitution of the United States."

The problem with the Bill of Rights, as with the Constitution itself, was that the rights and liberties of the people, as well as the duties, obligations, and limitations of the government had been reduced to words. Much of the debate in Congress during the drafting of the first ten amendments to the Constitution centered about the problem of defining a right without limiting it. A right, a freedom, or a liberty is more absolute when it is ill-defined; reducing any of these to words immediately places limits on it. The founding fathers knew with some degree of certainty what they envisioned the powers of the federal government to be when they drafted the Constitution, just as members of Congress knew what they intended in the Bill of Rights. Yet when these theories were reduced to words in the Constitution and later put into practice, meanings changed, just as the guaranteed freedoms would when later actual cases regarding them were tested in the courts.

Preserving, Protecting, and Defending

About ten o'clock on the morning of April 16, 1789, a fifty-seven year old Virginia farmer walked out the front door of his plantation home, entered his carriage, and set out for New York City. His was no simple pleasure trip, for on his shoulders rested the fate of a nation, the United States. To his diary he confided his thoughts that April morning: "I bade adieu to Mount Vernon, to private life, and to domestic felicity, and with a mind oppressed with more anxious and painful sensations than I have words to express, set out for New York...."

Ten days it took him to make the trip. Ten days it took, for everywhere the people sought to outdo each other in showing him their gratitude and respect. The road he followed was lined with multitudes of citizens; little girls dressed in white often preceded his carriage sprinkling flowers in its path. At every village the great man was met with parades, dinners, and fireworks, and gifts of every nature were pressed upon him. Yet inside his carriage he was acutely uncomfortable, for painful boils on his backside often forced him to lie flat on his stomach—while a contemplation of the state of the nation over which he was to preside brought long, sobering thoughts.

The newly formed United States stretched from the Atlantic Ocean to the Mississippi River and from Canada to Florida. It numbered fewer than 4,000,000 citizens, ninety-five percent of whom lived on farms; there was little manufacturing, the people depending on Europe for the most common items. From the government under the Articles of

Confederation the newly elected President would inherit little
and much. In terms of governmental machinery his legacy
was a Foreign Office headed by John Jay who, with his two
clerks, handled the correspondence with Thomas Jefferson in
Paris and John Adams in London—which constituted the
entire American diplomatic corps. He also inherited a
Secretary of War to direct the 840-man army and almost
nonexistent navy. Finally, he had the services of a dozen or so
clerks taking care of the rest of the government's business.

Also coming from the days of the Articles was a debt of
unknown proportions, an empty treasury, and no credit.
Many Americans openly were hoping the President and
government under the Constitution would fail. The poor
people of the nation feared the new government because it
had the power to tax them directly, while local and state
politicians were jealous that it might encroach on the power
and prestige which previously had been theirs. In the
southwest, particularly in Tennessee and Kentucky, talk of
secession was common; to the north, Vermonters openly
were negotiating with England for recognition as a separate
republic; and in between these extremes were two states,
North Carolina and Rhode Island, which as yet had not
ratified the Constitution. In the field of foreign affairs the
new republic was considered a joke; England was so
contemptuous of its former colony that it was maintaining
trading posts in the Northwest Territory which, by treaty, it
had ceded to the United States.

Finally, and perhaps most challenging, the United States
was divided into three major geographical areas, each of
which had little in common with the other. In the South the
rice and tobacco plantation owners, using slave labor, hated
and distrusted the merchants and ship-owners of the North,
while the food-growing farmers of the Middle States looked
with disdain on both of the other sections. Each of these
three areas was sufficiently large and unified to form single
nations. For this new President to secure the allegiance of all
to one government was a formidable task.

Yes, George Washington indeed faced a great challenge—
but his life had been filled with challenges which he had met
and overcome. He was born on February 22, 1732, at

Wakefield, his father's plantation in Westmoreland County, Virginia. After the death of his father, he lived with his elder half-brother Lawrence at Mount Vernon. Educated by his father and half-brother, he excelled in mathematics and surveying, although he gained an appreciation for music and drama, and read many books about history and military campaigns. As a member of one of the better families of Virginia, he moved in a society that stressed courtly manners, poise, and dignity until these became a part of his nature.

Arriving at manhood, he worked for a time as a surveyor, a task which took him into the wild back country. There followed a voyage to Barbados in the West Indies with Lawrence Washington. On this trip he was infected with smallpox, but survived to become immune thereafter (and thus was in no danger when the disease broke out among his troops during the Revolution). When Lawrence died in 1752, Mount Vernon passed into Washington's hands, and he undertook its management. That same year he was appointed a district adjutant in the colonial militia, and in the French and Indian Wars that followed he acquitted himself with distinction as a lieutenant colonel; to his diary in that period he confided, "I have heard the bullets whistle, and, believe me, there is something charming in the sound." Indeed he had, for in the attack on Fort Duquesne in 1755 he had four bullets through his coat and two horses shot from beneath him, but escaped untouched. By the end of that war he was commander in chief of Virginia's militia defending the western frontier from Indian attack.

In 1758 Washington married Martha Custis and returned to Mount Vernon as a gentleman farmer, serving from 1759 to 1774 as a member of the House of Burgesses. His fellow Virginians elected him to the First and Second Continental Congresses, by which time he was widely known and respected. He was not quick-witted and schooled in political theory, as were Jefferson and Hamilton; he was no deep scholar, as was Madison; nor was he a brilliant orator like Patrick Henry or a man of words like Thomas Paine. Rather Washington had that indefinable quality of leadership and the ability to inspire confidence that came from his solemn and dignified bearing, his good judgment, and, as one

Mount Vernon, a print published in London in 1800

contemporary said, his "common sense lifted to the level of genius." Captain George Mercer, who served as his aide in 1760 in the colonial militia, described him as more than six feet in height, 190 to 200 pounds, and large framed: "His bones and joints are large as are his hands and feet.... In conversation he looks you full in the face, is deliberate, deferential and engaging. His voice is agreeable." His friends stated that in private he was charming and personable, even "chatty" and on rare occasions "impudent." In public, however, he was reserved and solemn, a man of intense dignity.

On June 15, 1775, the Continental Congress asked him to assume command of the Continental Army. He accepted with reluctance, writing, "It is an honor I wished to avoid.... I can answer but for three things: a firm belief in the justice of our cause, close attention in the prosecution of it, and the strictest integrity." For some time his goal had been reconciliation with England; gradually, however, he had realized the necessity of the declaration of independence. During the war, saddled with raw troops, hampered by shortages of supplies and weapons, and criticized by bureaucrats who little appreciated his problems, he nevertheless achieved brilliant victories. In everything he gave credit to his soldiers: "Posterity will bestow on their labors the epithet and marks of fiction; for it will not be believed that such a force as Great Britain has employed for eight years in this country, could be baffled in their plan of subjugating it...." Yet it was Washington's leadership, his courage, his confidence, and his military genius that persisted until the triumph that ended at Yorktown was finally achieved.

The war over, he returned to Mount Vernon, stoutly resisting popular moves to proclaim him a dictator or king. When restive officers in the army talked of military revolution, he reproved them and ended the threat. During the next five years he enlarged his home at Mount Vernon, enjoyed his adopted children, served as an Episcopalian vestryman, and practiced scientific farming. But, also, he corresponded widely about the defects of the government under the Articles of Confederation, welcomed distinguished

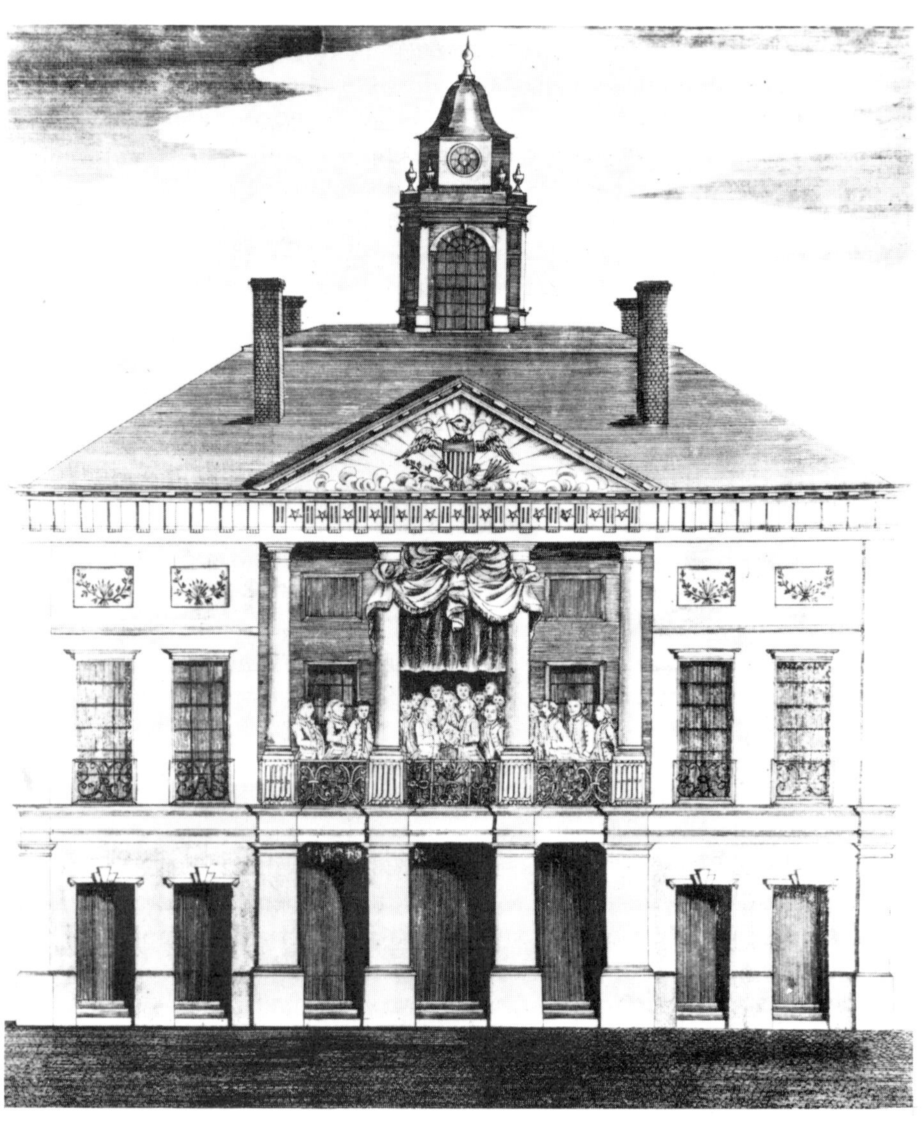

Federal Hall, the Seat of Congress

visitors at Mount Vernon, and hosted various gatherings. When the constitutional convention met in 1787 in Philadelphia, he reluctantly agreed to be a delegate from Virginia—and served as president of the meeting. The result, he felt, was "the best that could be obtained at this time," for it approached "nearer to perfection than any government hitherto instituted among men."

With the Constitution ratified, the public demand that Washington serve as the first President was so strong that everyone knew he would be elected. Voting in the electoral college was secret, but almost no American had doubts about the outcome. Congress was supposed to convene on March 4, 1789, and that day the guns on the Battery of Manhattan Island saluted the new government. Not until April 1, however, did the House of Representatives have a quorum, and five more days passed before the Senate had enough members present to do business. That day the two houses examined the ballots of the electoral college and declared Washington the winner by his sixty-nine ballots; John Adams, who had secured thirty-four votes, was to be the Vice-President. The man who had led the country through the war for independence now would have to guide the destiny of the young republic through its critical first years as a nation. When informed that the Presidency had been thrust upon him—he had not sought the office—he accepted at "the greatest sacrifice of my personal feeling and wishes." He added, "Integrity and firmness are all I can promise," for privately, he had doubts that he could administer the government as successfully as he had commanded the army. He feared appearing in public as incompetent and wrote; "My movements to the chair of government will be accompanied by feelings not unlike those of a culprit, who is going to the place of his execution."

Because he had invested so heavily in Continental bonds and securities during the Revolution, he was still in debt when elected President. Unwilling to leave his bills unpaid, he borrowed money both to pay these and his travel expenses to New York. There on April 30 at the old City Hall, which was serving as the temporary capitol, he took the oath of office at noon on a balcony overlooking the crowd of spectators.

Dressed in a brown suit and white stockings and with a
sword hanging at his side, he repeated the words in the
Constitution: *"I do solemnly swear that I will faithfully execute the
office of President of the United States and will, to the best of my ability,
preserve, protect, and defend the Constitution of the United States."* (This
site, later to become a sub-treasury building, today is marked
with a statue of Washington).

Once in office, Washington moved slowly, postponing
many matters until the machinery of government could be
perfected. Fortunately for the people of the United States,
and the new government, prosperity was returning. The
painful adjustments following the Revolution had been made.
The great wars connected with the French Revolution and
the Napoleonic era were beginning in 1789, so that for the
next several years American farm produce and raw products
commanded high prices overseas. Many citizens equated this
returning prosperity with the new government. Also, the
Washington administration had the backing of a favorable
press. And even its opponents, men such as Patrick Henry,
Samuel Adams, and Richard Henry Lee, were determined to
give it an opportunity. Finally, the new government was
largely in the hands of its friends; only one man in the first
Congress had opposed ratification of the Constitution, and
Washington's appointments, when they began to be made,
were strong Federalists.

Washington was aware that his first acts would set the
tenor of the republic for years to come: "...My station is
new," he confided to his diary, "and, if I may use the
expression, I walk on untrodden ground. There is scarcely an
action, the motive of which may not be subject to double
interpretation. There is scarcely any part of my conduct
which may not hereafter be drawn into precedent." Such was
the case in so minor a point as the method used for
addressing the chief executive. Washington preferred
something approaching that used by monarchs of Europe—
but settled for the democratic "Mr. President," the title still
used.

Another facet of his personality which influenced the
government was his unwillingness to come to vital decisions
without asking advice from men in whom he had confidence.

No doubt, this came from his military experience where he had a staff to assist him, but from it came the Cabinet, a body entirely different in origin and function from the British Cabinet. In the constitutional convention there had been talk of providing for a Privy Council to aid the President, but nothing was done. Apparently the framers of this document assumed that there would be different departments to handle foreign affairs, the army, and fiscal matters; references were made to this in the Constitution. As Congress created these departments, President Washington gradually turned to the department heads for advice, and they became his Cabinet.

The establishment of executive departments occupied much of the time of Congress that first session in the summer of 1789. While Congress debated, Washington continued to rely on the administrators he had inherited from the government under the Articles of Confederation: John Jay in Foreign Affairs, the old Treasury Board, and General Henry Knox in the War Department. Between July 27 and September 24 Congress created the departments of State, War, Treasury, Post Office, and Attorney General.

As Washington sought the men he wanted in each of these offices, he quite naturally turned to men whom he had seen tested during the Revolution, men whom he knew he could trust. Knowing that every appointment he made was critical, he wrote, "A single disgust excited in a particular State, on this account, might perhaps raise a flame of opposition.... Perfectly convinced I am, that if injudicious or unpopular measures should be taken by the executive under the new government, with regard to appointments, the government itself would be in the utmost danger of being utterly subverted by those measures." General Knox remained as Secretary of War; Alexander Hamilton became Secretary of the Treasury on September 11; Edmund Randolph was sworn into office as Attorney General on September 26, and shortly afterward Samuel Osgood became Postmaster General; not until March 22, 1790, however, did Thomas Jefferson return from France to assume the duties of Secretary of State.

When the first of these offices, State, was being created, the argument arose in Congress about the right of the

President to remove his appointees. Four different concepts were advanced during this debate: (1) that the President had the power to remove without consulting anyone; (2) that the power to remove was the same as the power to appoint and thus he needed the advice and consent of the Senate in such removals; (3) that each department was being created by Congress, and it set any requirements, such as requiring Senatorial advice and consent on removals, so long as these were not contrary to the Constitution; and (4) that a cabinet officer, once appointed, could be removed only by impeachment. James Madison fought in the House for the first option, saying, "It is one of the most prominent features of the Constitution, a principle that pervades the whole system, that there should be the highest possible degree of responsibility in all the Executive officers thereof; any thing, therefore, which tends to lessen this responsibility, is contrary to its spirit and intention. . . ." He concluded, "Vest this power in the Senate jointly with the President, and you abolish at once that great principle of unity and responsibility in the Executive department, which was intended for the security of liberty and the public good." By a final vote of thirty-one to nineteen the Senate agreed with the concept that the President could remove a cabinet officer without consulting that body.

Another quirk of Washington's personality that shaped the American government was his impatience. On August 22 he asked the Senate for advice and consent on a treaty with the Creek Indians. The Senate's sense of its dignity defeated its ambitions in this case, for it referred the matter to a committee. The President thereupon decided that henceforth he would submit only a signed treaty to the Senate for acceptance or rejection; he would not ask its advice during the treaty-making process. Since that summer of 1789, foreign affairs have been conducted solely by the President through the Department of State.

The third branch of government, the federal judiciary system, was established by Congress that year. On September 24 came the Federal Judiciary Act which provided for a Supreme Court, consisting of a Chief Justice and five Associate Justices; three circuit courts with two Supreme

Court justices per circuit; and thirteen district courts. The Constitution does not specify the number of justices serving on the Supreme Court, and subsequent sessions of Congress would see the number changed several times.

The most pressing need of the new government, however, was not for departments to be created or even for courts to be established, but rather for money. On April 8, 1789, just two days after both houses had a quorum, they began debating a tariff measure. Signed on July 4—to take effect on August 1—this measure provided a ten-percent discount on the duty of goods imported in American ships. Next came an act levying a tonnage duty on all ships entering American ports: six cents per ton on American ships, twenty cents per ton on ships built in the United States but registered in a foreign country, and fifty cents per ton on all other ships. These measures not only raised desperately needed revenue for the national treasury, but also they helped revive American shipping. Together the two acts provided some protection for American manufacturers, stimulated shipbuilding, and pleased New Englanders greatly.

In his first message to Congress, President Washington had stated that he wished no salary as chief executive. However, Congress did vote him $25,000 annually—and he accepted it to help defray his expenses as President; in fact, he spent more than this every year entertaining and traveling. He knew that to get the various regions of the United States to accept the concept of a national government he had to popularize it. Thus when Congress adjourned in September 1789, he set out on a tour of the New England states. Governor John Hancock of Massachusetts, an Anti-Federalist, sought to diminish the importance of the President's visit and to embarrass Washington, but the citizens proved that they wanted to see the President and welcomed him warmly. Well might Washington write, as he did early in 1790, that "the Government, though not absolutely perfect, is one of the best in the world...."

The first priority of the new government was the need to attain fiscal stability. Following this in importance was the necessity of forcing the British to abide by the provisions of the treaty that had ended the Revolution, especially with

regard to abandoning their trading posts in the Northwest
Territory. As a result of the need to raise money, the
government regulated and restricted commerce. As a result of
the second, it became embroiled in foreign affairs.

Alexander Hamilton as Secretary of the Treasury and as
one of George Washington's closest confidants had the
responsibility of drafting a fiscal report that would guide
Congress in its deliberations. In fact, Hamilton assumed the
task of administrative spokesman in Congress, attending
committee meetings, exercising his personal influence with
members of the legislative branch, and lobbying to secure
their votes. In 1790 and 1791 he drafted four great proposals
regarding the fiscal stance he thought the republic should
take; two of these were devoted to public credit, one to
banking, and one to manufacturing; out of these were
extracted specific legislation for Congress to pass. In these
four reports and the resulting legislation, Hamilton showed
his political philosophy. He believed in a strong national
government which was to operate for the benefit of the
upper class: property owners, merchants, financiers,
manufacturers, and the great land owners. If the government
promoted the well-being of these men, Hamilton reasoned,
they in turn would support the government.

Opposition to the Hamilton program came from Thomas
Jefferson, who favored the yeoman farmer (small land owners
who had the vote), a small national government with most
power retained by the states, and the creditor class. In foreign
policy Hamilton favored England, while Jefferson was an
admirer of France. Within this contest over internal and
foreign policies was born the two political parties that would
flower during Washington's presidency—and then fight for
supremacy for two decades: the Federalists (Hamilton) and
the Democrat-Republicans (Jefferson).

Hamilton's report on payment of the public debt and the
establishment of American credit was delivered to Congress
on January 14, 1790. In this he proposed paying the national
debt at face value; at this time the national debt, including
interest, stood at $11,710,378 owed to foreign nations and
$42,414,085 to Americans. "If all the public creditors receive
their dues from one source distributed with an equal hand,"

Hamilton reasoned, "... they will unite in support of the fiscal arrangements of the government." He suggested that all creditors exchange their old notes for new bonds which, in time, would be paid at full value. Madison strongly opposed paying the domestic debt at face value, for this would work to the benefit of speculators who had bought up Continental bonds at a fraction of their value. Southerners opposed Hamilton's plan, for it called for the federal government to pay off state debts incurred on behalf of the Revolution; most Southern states had already paid these, leaving the Northern states to benefit most from this proposal. This fight over federal fiscal policy was settled at a dinner at Jefferson's home. Hamilton and the Northerners agreed to locate the permanent capital of the United States in the south, on the Potomac, in return for support for the funding bill. Thus on August 4 the Funding Act was passed, and the First Congress could adjourn with positive action taken.

The Second Congress convened for its first session in Philadelphia on December 6, 1790. Philadelphia would remain the capital until 1800 when the city established in the District of Columbia was ready to receive the government. A week after Congress convened, Hamilton presented his second report, a call for a National Bank. This recommendation proposed a Bank of the United States capitalized at $10 million, the federal government providing twenty per cent of the money and private sources contributing the remaining eighty percent. The bank would serve as depository for federal funds, its notes would be the nation's principal currency, and it would assist the government in funding the debt. In addition, it would perform other normal banking functions. Despite heavy Southern opposition, led by Madison, the House passed the bill on February 8 by a vote of thirty-nine to twenty; thirty-three of the positive votes came from Northerners, whose region stood to profit most. During debate on the measure in the Senate, Jefferson made known his opposition, arguing the doctrine of strict interpretation of the constitution; nothing in the constitution specifically authorized the government to establish a bank, and therefore to create one would be unconstitutional. Hamilton replied on February 23, arguing a loose construction of the constitution;

The Bank of the United States

under the "necessary and proper" clause, Hamilton reasoned, the government had the authority to create a bank. The Senate agreed with Hamilton, and on February 25 Washington signed the bank bill, which chartered the Bank for twenty years, to be headquartered in Philadelphia.

This debate had long-lasting consequences. The Bank of the United States would be an issue for almost half a century, while the "strict construction" versus "loose construction" of the constitution would be a rallying cry for those favoring a large federal government against those who believed in states' rights—an issue still much alive in the United States. In the immediate aftermath of passage of the Bank bill in 1791, the issues raised would serve to polarize opinions and divide Americans into two political camps: Hamiltonians (or Federalists, as they were better known) and Jeffersonians (or Democrat-Republicans as they came to be known). In short, political parties were born from this debate.

Hamilton's third recommendation was passage of an act to collect excise taxes on various commodities, especially distilled liquors. Congress agreed, passing the measure on March 3, 1791, with little debate. Thus when stock in the Bank of the United States was offered to the public on July 4, 1791, it was sold entirely within one hour. Faith in the credit of the United States was high. Hamilton presented his final recommendation on American fiscal policies on December 5, 1791, a "Report on Manufactures," in which he urged a protective tariff to encourage American manufacturing, bounties to farmers growing specified crops, and federal spending for internal improvements. Hamilton's program in its entirety—a Bank, funding the public debt to be paid at face value by the federal government, excise taxes, a protective tariff, bounties to help agriculture, and internal improvements—committed his followers, the Federalists, to these goals; in short, Hamilton had written the platform for the Federalists and, after that party dissolved, for the Whig Party, which would last until the 1850's. These were the goals of New Englanders committed to manufacturing and commerce.

Resistance to the excise tax on whiskey began in August, 1792, in North Carolina and western Pennsylvania. Farmers found corn bulky and hard to transport, therefore they converted it into whiskey for easy shipment to market. This practice was so standard that whiskey had become a medium of exchange in several parts of the nation. Thus a tax on whiskey seemed a tax on money itself, and objections led to the shooting of tax collectors. Another feature of the law very objectionable to farmers was that violators of this law were to be tried in federal court. In Pennsylvania the federal court sat at Philadelphia, 350 miles from Pittsburgh, the scene of much whiskey-making. The trip itself was a costly fine, even though an accused man might be found innocent.

Despite the unrest created by the excise tax, Washington knew he could have a second term as President just by accepting it. Personally he would have preferred to retire to Mount Vernon, for he was beginning to feel old age setting in. To Thomas Jefferson during his first term, he confided that he was "growing old, his bodily health less firm, his memory, always bad, becoming worse, and perhaps the other faculties of his mind showing a decay to others of which he was insensible himself." He had gained a few critics of the pomp and ceremony with which he had invested the office of President; Anti-Federalists denounced him as a would-be king because of his formal dignity, his regal bearing, and the trappings of office he insisted upon having. However, Washington knew that some ceremony was necessary to lend dignity and authority to the new government, both internally and externally. He gave voice to this thought in his fifth annual message to Congress: "There is a rank due to the United States among nations, which will be withheld if not absolutely lost, by the reputation of weakness."

Despite ill-health and his critics, Washington did choose to accept a second term, and on December 5, 1792, he received 132 electoral votes. Adams was re-elected Vice-President with seventy-seven electoral votes, while George Clinton, a supporter of Jefferson, received fifty votes for the vice-presidency.

Early in Washington's second term, the major concern of the nation became foreign, not domestic, affairs. Inspired in part by the American example, the French Revolution swept that nation beginning in 1789 and ending on September 21,

1792, with the proclamation of a republic. At first Americans warmly supported their French cousins in what seemed a parallel experience. However, early in 1793 Louis XVI was executed, followed by the infamous "Reign of Terror" that saw the guillotine stifling dissent. Conservative Americans, especially the Hamiltonians, turned against the French Revolution, while the Jeffersonians still maintained sympathy for it while deploring its excesses. On February 1, 1793, France declared war on England, Spain, and Holland in an attempt to extend its boundaries and its doctrines. Because the United States was exporting goods to France and to England, the government was faced with making a choice between them. Hamilton exerted his influence on Washington to favor Great Britain, while Jefferson used his persuasive powers to make the president favor France.

This dispute came to a head when on April 8, 1793, Edmond Charles Genêt intrigued with Americans to attack Spanish Florida and Louisiana and he issued letters commissioning privateers to attack British shipping. Meanwhile, in Philadelphia, Jefferson argued to the president that the American treaty of 1778 with France obligated the United States to defend the French West Indies and to receive prize ships captured on the seas. Hamilton countered with the argument that the treaty of 1778 was with the royalist government and that the United States should side with England to defeat the Republicans. Washington responded to these arguments with a Neutrality Proclamation on April 22, and he received Genet with distinct coldness and a statement that he would tolerate no violations of neutrality. Genet persisted in his activities, believing that the majority of Americans were with him, whereupon Washington, on August 23, demanded that he be recalled by his government. By this time, however, Genêt's group was in disfavor in France, and he asked to be allowed to stay in the United States. His request was granted.

Americans profited greatly from the European conflict as its exports of food and other materials commanded premium prices. With the French fleet at the mercy of England's naval superiority, the French government threw the West Indies open to American shipping. England retaliated by declaring

food to be contraband (a material of war) and began seizing
American ships. The American government reiterated its
declaration of neutrality and asserted that neutral ships made
neutral goods, especially in the case of food. By the spring of
1794 some three hundred American ships had been seized by
England, and even the Federalists, who favored conciliation
with England, believed war was imminent. Moreover, the
British had refused to return many of the northwestern posts
on American soil to American control; and the Canadian
Governor-General, Lord Dorchester, chose that time to incite
the Indians of the Northwest to raid in the Ohio country. The
Jeffersonian Republicans demanded that Congress pass
commercial retaliatory laws against England—that British
ships be embargoed from American ports and that American
ships be kept from trading with England. In April, by a close
vote, the measure passed Congress, to be in effect for one
month (subsequently it was extended two months).

President Washington favored diplomacy to settle the
growing problems with England, and on April 16, 1794,
named Chief Justice John Jay a special envoy to Great Britain
to negotiate points of difference between the two nations.
That fall Jay found his position somewhat strengthened by
General Anthony Wayne's defeat of the Indians in the Ohio
country at the Battle of Fallen Timbers on August 20. Jay
thus began negotiating to secure British surrender of the
posts in the Northwest Territory, British indemnity for
American ships they had captured, and British recognition of
the rights of neutrals. There was talk that if England failed to
agree to these demands, Jay was to proceed to Sweden and
Denmark to discuss with them a combined assault on
Britain's failure to respect neutrality. However, Alexander
Hamilton was so pro-British that he informed them of
Washington's secret decision not to join the Swedes and
Danes in armed neutrality against England, and thus Jay
failed to gain concessions that might have resulted.

On November 19 the Treaty of London was signed
between the United States and England. Known in America
as Jay's Treaty, this instrument provided for British
evacuation of the Northwest posts, although it stipulated that
Canadians could still trap furs south of the border and trade

with the Indians; a joint commission was created to discuss payment for captured American ships; and Americans could trade with England on a most-favored-nation basis, as well as trade without discrimination in the British East Indies. Jay failed to get the British to recognize the rights of neutrals on the high seas, and the British continued to stop and search American ships, just as they continued to force many crewmen on American vessels into British naval service (a practice known as impressment).

Jay's Treaty was greeted in America with a loud outcry of public indignation. Washington, after long hesitation, sent it to the Senate with his endorsement, and that body ratified it on June 25 by a slender two-thirds majority. Even Hamilton's series of newspaper articles signed "Camillus" in defense of the treaty did not allay public indignation, and Jay was hanged in effigy in many places in the country.

Spain, meanwhile, had reconsidered its alliance with England against France and made peace with the revolutionary government of its neighbor to the north. Fearful of attacks by American frontiersmen on its New World colonies, Spanish officials determined to make concessions to the United States in return for friendship and peace. Thomas Pinckney, American minister to England, went to Spain and there on October 27, 1795, signed the Treaty of San Lorenzo. This instrument, known as Pinckney's Treaty, stipulated the 31st parallel as the boundary between Florida and Georgia, and granted Americans free navigation of the Mississippi River "in its whole length" and free use of the port of New Orleans for three years (with provisions for extending the time period). Pinckney's Treaty was enthusiastically received in America, especially by frontiersmen who found it much easier to transport their goods to the Eastern seaboard by way of the Mississippi.

Internal and external policies of the Washington administration coincided during his second term on the matter of excise taxes. Despite the opposition to this tax which had arisen during Washington's first term, Hamilton as Secretary of the Treasury argued that collections should continue to convince foreign powers that a republic could make its citizens show financial responsibility; otherwise the public credit of the United States might collapse. By 1794 opposition to the excise tax on whiskey had risen to such heights that receipts from it had fallen below the cost of collection. That summer, when federal marshals attempted to arrest violators, they were attacked by irate farmers and distillers. Hamilton persuaded Washington that such attacks were rebellion against the United States, and on August 7 the President issued a proclamation ordering the rebels to return to their homes and calling out 13,000 militiamen from four states to suppress the uprising against federal authority. Washington himself accompanied the troops as far west as Carlisle, Pennsylvania, while Hamilton, who had dreams of martial glory, rode all the way with them. The show of force caused the "Whiskey Rebellion" to collapse. About one hundred men were arrested by the militia, and two men were convicted of treason. They were sentenced to death, but Washington pardoned them. This show of force did much to advance the standing of the federal government, both at home and abroad. Internally it demonstrated the effectiveness of the national government (as opposed to the government under the Articles of Confederation), by showing that the new government would enforce its laws. Abroad it demonstrated that the government could make its citizens pay their taxes, and thereby strengthened the credit of the United States.

George Washington had seriously considered retiring at the end of his first term in office and had asked Madison and others to draft suggestions for a farewell address. In 1796 he used these suggestions to prepare such a paper, which was not delivered in person but published in the newspapers on September 17, 1796. In this valedictory to the nation, Washington warned the nation against political parties, especially those based on geographical grounds *"Northern* and *Southern, Atlantic* and *Western."* Instead, he urged a "unity of government which constitutes you one people." On foreign policy, he stressed "extending our commercial relations to have with them as little political connection as possible," for "temporary alliances for extraordinary emergencies" could always be established. "As a very important source of strength and security," he wrote, "cherish public credit. One method of preserving it is to use it as sparingly as possible, avoiding occasions of expense by cultivating peace, but remembering also that timely disbursements to prepare for danger frequently prevent much greater disbursements to repel it."

He thus did not argue against "entangling alliances," but for commercial ties. His advice on this score would not be remembered, just as was forgotten his wisdom on the score of public credit. His retirement after two terms did establish a precedent that would be broken only once in American history.

During his eight years in office, Washington's chief goal had been to strengthen the nation, to unify the people, to dissolve local prejudice, and to gain for the country the international standing he felt it deserved. Hamilton's financial program helped, in part, attain these ends, as did the strengthening of the army and navy and the treaties made abroad. The wars with the Indians and the enforcement of the national taxing powers did yet more to achieve the same goals. In this process he had established procedures for conducting the government and had set a pattern of administration that future Presidents would follow. He was venerated during his own lifetime for his contributions during the Revolution; later Americans owe him far more for his role in the crucial years immediately following the ratification of the Constitution.

Despite the place he knew he had secured for himself in future history books, Washington remained an unpretentious man. Rufus King of Massachusetts, who watched the inauguration of Washington's successor as President in March of 1797, wrote of him as he came to turn over the reins of government, "He came unattended and on foot, with the modest appearance of a private citizen." This same letter shows that despite the criticism he had received, Washington was still very much the favorite of common people: "No sooner was his person seen, than a burst of applause such as I had never before known, and which it would be as impossible for me to describe, as my own sensations produced by it, saluted the venerable Hero and Patriot. . . ."

John Adams installed in office, Washington at last could

retire to his plantation of Mount Vernon secure in the
knowledge that the government of the nation had been
established on a firm foundation. His years of retirement
were few, however, for he died in 1799. In the weeks that
followed his death, a torrent of tribute flowed in state
legislatures, Congress, and town meetings. Funeral
enactments occurred in more than two hundred towns, as
Americans vied to express their grief at the passing of the
hero "First in war, first in peace, and first in the hearts of his
countrymen." That phrase, so often repeated, reveals facts
about Washington not usually remembered. He was, first and
foremost, the soldier who had won the American Revolution;
yet as President much of his time was consumed in keeping
the infant nation out of the European vortex of conflict
stirred by the French Revolution; and he was probably the
most popular American, within his own time, who ever lived.
Friends and enemies alike agreed on this score. He was a
great man, a good man, and a human man—one still worthy
of imitation, one whose precepts for government still bear
heeding.

Present-day Americans might well argue that
Washington's greatest legacy was not his service during the
Revolution, but rather his years as President. As chief
executive of the young nation he balanced the great dilemma
of democracy: maximum freedom and domestic order. He
provided a stable government, but one where individual
liberties were respected. Even more important—he
established a climate where revolution could continue; all men
were not equal before the law in Washington's day, but he
helped institutionalize a system of legal change that has
continued for two hundred years.

"Famous Whiskey Insurrection in Pennsylvania"

132

Evolution of the Miracle

8

By 1796, when George Washington announced that he would not accept a third term as President, the United States had all the elements for a continuing revolution, one that would gradually bring it closer to the ideals for which it had separated from England. During that conflict Thomas Jefferson had drafted a statement about the natural rights of man and an assertion of why governments were instituted. This Declaration constituted the underlying philosophy of the United States. However, owing to the conditions then prevailing, the founding fathers had to compromise those ideals somewhat, for government then was in the hands of the propertied few. Nevertheless, these men did try to institutionalize the ideals of the Declaration of Independence in the Constitution—and they did this without regard to race except for the three-fifths compromise and the statement about the importation of slaves for twenty years.

The Declaration of Independence was idealistic, the Constitution practical. The one sang, the other plodded. One principally was the work of Thomas Jefferson, the other of James Madison. Jefferson, a follower of Rousseau, believed that the general will of the people should rule a country; Madison, who was infatuated with the beliefs of Montesquieu, argued that the separation of powers was necessary to prevent a republican government from degenerating into tyranny. Both the Declaration and the Constitution were necessary in forming the government of the United States, one bespeaking a concern for the rights of man and the other a blueprint for government. Without the

John Adams

Declaration, the Constitution would have been little more than a collection of "whereases" and "wherefores"; for this reason it was necessary to add the Bill of Rights—which really is nothing more than a restatement of the Declaration of Independence. These two concepts, idealism and practicality, have become the essence of Americanism. One says what the law ought to be, while the other tempers the ideal with reality. In the two hundred years since the founding of the republic, the history of the United States has been one long attempt to bring the practical into philosophical balance with the ideal.

In 1789, when the United States began under its present government, few would have argued that the ideal had been implemented. Voting and office holding were confined to the wealthy, especially to landowners: farmers in New England, the plantation owners of the South, the patroons of New York, the Germans of Pennsylvania, the owners of property in the cities. Others with a voice in society in 1789 were the shipowners and shipbuilders, the merchants and businessmen, lawyers and doctors, former officers of the Revolutionary Army, and the clergy. In several states anyone wanting to vote had to belong to a certain church, hold property of a certain value, and have a specified income annually.

Yet Thomas Jefferson, who owned slaves, had written, "All men are created equal." The Constitution was drafted in such a way that the franchise could be expanded as needed. Washington had headed a government where legislative, judicial, and executive powers were separated, one where the idealistic could legislate but be tempered by the practicality of the Constitution—and all would be put into effect by the executive branch. In short, the country had a philosophical and practical basis whereby the forces of change could exert themselves in an atmosphere of constitutional benevolence. There was no need for civil war, for a continuing revolution was legal.

During Washington's administration two attitudes had contended with one another. Led by Alexander Hamilton, one faction had fought to preserve rule by the wealthy, while the other faction, led by Thomas Jefferson, wanted the small

farmers and the laboring class to be participating members of
the government. These two factions had evolved into political
parties, the Federalists and the Democrat-Republicans,
although the Constitution had made no provision for such an
event. In the election of 1796 the Federalists named John
Adams of Massachusetts as their candidate for President and
Thomas Pinckney, who was popular because of his treaty
with Spain, for Vice-President. The Democrat-Republicans
responded by naming Thomas Jefferson for President with
Aaron Burr of New York as his running mate. Hamilton, who
disliked Adams, worked for the election of Pinckney, a
scheme that brought Adams to the presidency with seventy-
one electoral votes and Jefferson to the vice-presidency with
sixty-eight votes. The result was an increase in partisan
rivalry. Republicans, as members of Jefferson's party
increasingly called themselves, characterized Adams as a
"three-vote president," a phrase that infuriated him.

Adams although tactless, unattractive, and cold was
experienced in foreign affairs and diplomacy. He was
intelligent, well-educated, master of four languages, and
owned perhaps the largest private library in America at this
time. Yet for all his wisdom, he was a poor judge of
character—and a man whose hatred for his opponents led him
to jail as many Republicans as possible. He did this under
terms of the Alien and Sedition Acts, four measures designed
to stifle discontent. In the end his high-handed techniques
caused followers of Hamilton to abandon him. In 1800 he and
his running mate, Charles C. Pinckney of South Carolina,
were defeated. Jefferson was elected to the presidency and
Aaron Burr to the vice-presidency (after a tie vote in the
electoral college that led to the addition of the twelfth
amendment; this specifies that members of the electoral
college will vote first—and separately—for President and then
for Vice-President).

In his inaugural address Jefferson indicated the type of
government he intended to administer: equal and exact justice
for all men; peace, commerce, and honest friendship with all
nations, entangling alliances with none; support of state
governments in their rights; the right of the people to elect
their officials; supremacy of civil over military authority; a

well-disciplined militia; and economy in public expenditures. In the national government, now headquartered in Washington, D.C., he introduced simplicity into the social life by affecting rustic dress and a casual pose in public. Jefferson idealized agriculture as a way of life for he believed it developed moral and political virtue. The secretary of the British legation in Washington wrote that the President looked like "a tall, large-boned farmer."

During his eight years in office Jefferson could count many positive achievements both in domestic and foreign affairs. Yet he was particularly proud of two accomplishments, both having to do with land and the way the people could acquire it—and thereby the vote. When the United States came into existence under the government of the Articles, one of its few assets was land; in dire need of money, that government devised a policy designed to raise revenue. The Land Ordinance of 1785, the first official American policy dealing with the public domain, had provided for the sale of land at public auction in minimum blocks of 640 acres at a minimum cash price of one dollar per acre. Yet sales were slow, for few actual settlers could afford the cash price.

The next basic change in policy came eleven years later. Alexander Hamilton, when Secretary of the Treasury, had urged that the government use its huge holdings of public lands to raise revenue. The result was the Act of 1796 which retained the 640-acre minimum but raised the cash price to two dollars per acre; the intent of this minimum price was to discourage speculators, who had been profiting hugely by purchasing large blocks of land and then breaking it up for sale to actual settlers. Realizing that few yeoman farmers had $1280 in cash, Congress did provide for extending credit: one-twentieth of the cash price had to be paid at the time of the sale, nine-twentieths to be paid within thirty days, and the remaining one-half to be paid within an additional year. The Act of 1796 actually discouraged the sale of land, for in the next four years less than 50,000 acres were sold.

By 1800 Congressmen realized that a change was necessary, for little revenue was flowing into the federal treasury from the sale of land. The Act of that year reduced

An engraving showing the impressment of American sailors by the British, dated April 28, 1806.

the minimum amount of each purchase of 320 acres at a minimum of two dollars per acre, and provided more liberal credit terms: one-fourth within forty days, another one-fourth within two years, and the remaining one-half within four years from the date of sale, with the indebtedness bearing an interest of six percent annually.

At the behest of Thomas Jefferson, Congress in 1804 passed an act providing for sale of specified lands (in Indiana and other places) at a cash price of $1.64 per acre or $1.84 per acre on credit, and reduced the minimum size of a purchase to 160 acres—the credit system remained unaltered. By the terms of this act an actual settler could acquire 160 acres for less than three hundred dollars, which meant he had to have only some seventy-five dollars in cash to acquire a subsistence farm. Obviously this system allowed many more people to acquire farms—and thereby the right to vote. Thereby Jefferson was instrumental in changing the basic philosophy of the federal government's land policy; thereafter the basic purpose of land sales was not to raise revenue—although the money did help the treasury balance—but rather to increase the number of voters.

As President, Jefferson overcame some of his feelings about the strict construction of the Constitution when faced with the opportunity to add millions of acres to the public domain by the purchase of the Louisiana Territory. This purchase was made possible by events in Europe during the Napoleonic wars. Napoleon had risen to power late in the 1790s and dreamed of reestablishing the French empire. Attempting to achieve this goal, he forced the weak and corrupt Spanish government to retrocede the Louisiana Territory to France by the secret Treaty of San Ildefonso on October 1, 1800. He then dispatched an army of 27,000 men to occupy Louisiana and, on the way there, to stop in Haiti and suppress an insurrection of slaves. Unfortunately for Napoleon's dreams of empire, his army was decimated in Haiti by yellow fever and the rebelling slaves. Short of men and pressed by his European involvement, he could not send another army to Louisiana.

Meanwhile, Jefferson had heard of the secret Treaty of San Ildefonso and watched with anxiety. Spanish officials had

been sharply curtailing the American right of transit on the
Mississippi and the right to deposit goods at New Orleans.
The President therefore in January 1803 asked the Senate to
name James Monroe as minister extraordinary, with
authority to work with the American minister to France, to
seek the purchase of the port city of New Orleans from
Napoleon. The Senate concurred with this request, and
Congress obligingly voted $2,000,000 for such a purchase.
When Monroe arrived in France, he discovered that the
French shortage of troops and their war with England had
worked to the American advantage. Napoleon now could not
occupy Louisiana—and if he kept title to it the British
doubtless would take it. Thus when the American ministers
approached the French government on April 11, 1803, they
were astonished to be offered all of Louisiana. With no time
to consult with Jefferson, for Napoleon wished to move
quickly, the American ministers arrived at a price of
$15,000,000 and the treaty of purchase was drawn and signed
on April 30, 1803. "We have lived long," stated Robert
Livingston, the American minister to France, "but this is the
noblest work of our lives."

That noble work proved a headache to Jefferson when
the treaty arrived in Washington, for as a strict
constructionist of the Constitution, he could find nothing in
that document which authorized the government to acquire
new territory. At first he considered a constitutional
amendment to authorize the purchase, but that took too
much time. Jefferson therefore swallowed his constitutional
qualms and simply sent the treaty to the Senate for
ratification. The Senate concurred with his judgment and
ratified the agreement in October 1803. There then arose a
second obstacle: the Constitution stated that a treaty was the
law of the land, yet it also stated that money bills should
originate in the House—and the Louisiana treaty obligated
the United States to pay France $15,000,000. Fortunately the
House concurred and voted the money, and a crisis was
averted. Then, by a stroke of his pen, Thomas Jefferson
doubled the size of the United States, thereby insuring that
the revolution would continue; more men would become
"equal" in the sense of the Declaration of Independence, for

they would, by acquiring land, become participants in the democratic process.

In the years following Thomas Jefferson's two terms in office, the United States changed rapidly—and dramatically. Two Virginians followed as President, James Madison and James Monroe, during which time the Federalist Party ceased to exist; in 1816 that party managed to nominate a candidate, Rufus King of New York, but he had no real chance of election. By 1820, when Monroe ran for reelection, he had no opposition and secured every electoral vote except one. Other changes occurring in this era included the extension of the suffrage. Property requirements for the franchise fell by the wayside as several states drafted new constitutions. By 1830 only three states legally were not granting universal white, male suffrage, and voter participation in state elections reached eighty percent and more.

Following the War of 1812 came widespread acceptance of mechanized industry, some economic independence from Europe, and protective tariffs guaranteed the future of American industries. Turnpikes were constructed, and the Erie Canal was built between 1817 and 1825 to link the Hudson River with the Great Lakes. These roads and canals not only promoted rapid transport but also the opening of the frontier region to settlers. Several new states were added to the Union: Tennessee, Kentucky, Ohio, Alabama, Mississippi, Indiana, Illinois, Missouri, and Louisiana, along with Vermont and Maine. Markets expanded with the western settlement, which, combined with the growth of factories, brought increased employment in manufacturing—and even the beginnings of labor unions. Tens of thousands of Europeans rushed to the New World to find better jobs and a new life.

These events changed the American people. At the turn of the nineteenth century, several commentators had written that Americans were given to sloth and idleness; George White stated that Americans were "apt, for want of due encouragement to industrious habits, to throw away their time in worse than useless idleness and dissipation." By the late 1820s, when Francis Grund immigrated from Austria, he could comment, "The United States presents certainly the most animated picture of universal bustle and activity of any country in the world. Such a thing as rest or quiescence does not even enter the mind of an American...." Even the leisure of Americans, he noted, consisted of nervous activity: rocking, chewing, whittling. These restless, striving people were quick to accept anything new; Frederick List, a German economist visiting the United States in the 1820s, wrote, "...Everything new is quickly introduced here, and all the latest inventions. There is no clinging to the old ways; the moment an American hears the word 'invention' he pricks up his ears." In short, America was adopting the concept of progress.

Two areas in which this surge of activity, of change, of ferment was being reflected were in the method of selecting presidential electors in the states and legislative apportionment. Settlers in the back country of every state were demanding increased representation in the legislatures and a direct voice in choosing presidential electors rather than have these chosen in the legislatures. Conservatives fought these changes, for they realized that a President elected directly by the people would be answerable to a wide constituency, not just to a few party members most of whom already were in Congress. By 1840 only South Carolina was still choosing its electors in the state legislature. Alexis de Tocqueville, who visited the United States in 1835, wrote, "...The political activity which pervades the United States must be seen in order to be understood. No sooner do you set foot upon American ground, than you are stunned by a kind of tumult....Almost the only pleasure which an American knows is to take a part in the government, and to discuss its measures."

Old Federalists noted these changes with horror. Chancellor James Kent of New York, participating in a constitutional convention in his state in 1821, spoke against universal adult, white male suffrage by stating, "That extreme principle...has been regarded with terror, by the wise men of every age, because in every European republic, ancient and modern, in which it has been tried, it has terminated disastrously and been productive of corruption, injustice, violence, and tyranny." Warming to his task, he asserted that "there is a tendency in the poor to covet and to share the plunder of the rich; in the debtor to relax or avoid the obligation of contracts;... in the indolent and profligate to cast the whole burden of society upon the industrious and virtuous...."

In the midst of this change—and the conservative reaction against it—came the election of 1824. That year there were too many candidates, for Monroe left the prize to no specified heir. New Englanders united behind John Quincy Adams, while Carolinians wanted John Calhoun; Henry Clay, Speaker of the House of Representatives, had the backing of Kentucky, while Andrew Jackson, hero of New Orleans and Florida, had mass public appeal. Then, to the astonishment of the public, the Democrat-Republican Party (which increasingly was dropping "Republican" from its name, to be called the Democratic Party) in the party caucus in Washington, nominated Secretary of the Treasury William H. Crawford of Georgia. Seemingly that year every legislature, every state party caucus, even militiamen meeting to drill on weekends, was naming a presidential candidate.

The followers of each contender became engaged in endless intrigue, trying to get one of the other nominees to accept the vice-presidential slot on the ballot, for victory seemingly would be assured if two men would combine on one ticket. John Calhoun did agree to a slate that included Jackson for the top office and himself for the second position. The popular vote in that election was difficult to determine, for electors in six states were still chosen by state legislatures, and in other states not all candidates were listed on the ballot; a rough approximation showed Jackson receiving 153,000 votes, Adams 108,000, Clay 47,000, and Crawford 46,000. In the Electoral College—the tally that really counted—Jackson had ninety-nine votes, Adams eighty-four, Crawford forty-one, and Clay thirty-seven. Because no candidate had a majority, the election was thrown into the House of Representatives where the race automatically was narrowed to the top three contenders.

Clay, who ran fourth and thus had been eliminated, was in a position of strength. His support would elect the next President. He was known to disagree with the policies of Crawford, and he hated Jackson. Just before the House voted,

Chancellor James Kent

Henry Clay

John Quincy Adams

it became public knowledge that Clay had an interview with
Adams, and he announced that he would support the
candidate from Massachusetts. The result was the election of
Adams to the presidency—whereupon Adams named Clay
Secretary of State. Jackson's bitter followers immediately
cried that a "deal" had been made: Clay's support in return
for his being named Secretary of State, which then was
considered the next step to the presidency.

Immediately after the election of 1824 ended, the
campaign for the presidency in 1828 began. Jackson's
followers cried that a "corrupt bargain" had cheated the
people of the United States of their choice for President, and
in the next four years they postured their man as a hero of
the common people. This was easy to do because of Jackson's
background and stormy rise to fame.

Born in rural South Carolina on March 15, 1767, of Irish
immigrant parents, Jackson was orphaned early. His father
died just before his third son was born, while his mother died
of illness during the American Revolution. During that war,
young Jackson served the Patriot side as a mounted courier,
and afterward moved to North Carolina where he was
admitted to the bar at age twenty. The following year he
moved west to Nashville, Tennessee, as public prosecutor for
the western district. Dabbling in land and slave speculation,
he prospered. There he met Rachel Donelson Robards, who
recently had been granted a divorce by the Virginia
legislature, and they were married in 1792. Only later—to
their horror and astonishment—did they learn that Rachel's
divorce was not final until 1793; once they knew this fact,
they immediately remarried, but the charge living in adultery
for more than two years plagued the two. On several
occasions Jackson resorted to dueling and horsewhipping his
enemies over this, as well as for political reasons, giving him a
reputation for violence and an iron will.

When Tennessee became a state, Jackson was elected to
Congress in 1796 and to the Senate the following year;
however, in 1798 he resigned to accept a position as judge on
the superior court of his home state. After serving there for
six years, he retired to develop his farm and home, known as
the Hermitage. When the War of 1812 began, he was

Andrew Jackson

(drawn and engraved by J. B. Longacre)

commissioned a major general of the Tennessee volunteers. As a result of his grim determination during this conflict, he became known as "Old Hickory," emerging from the war a national hero because of his victories at the battles of Horseshoe Bend and New Orleans. He won additional glory in 1817 when, as a major general in the regular army, he invaded Florida where he defeated the Spaniards, their English advisors, and their Indian allies. This forced Spain in 1819 to cede Florida to the United States. Jackson then resigned his commission in 1821 to become governor of Florida, only to quit that post six months later owing to displeasure with President Monroe, who had criticized the invasion of Florida. In 1823 Jackson returned to the Senate.

By that time he already was being pushed for the presidency in 1824. When Adams secured the position, Jackson and his followers shouted what became almost a national belief among the common people: the Hero of New Orleans had been cheated, as had the will of the majority of Americans; the aristocratic people and high politicians had conspired to defeat the voters' choice. When at last the election of 1828 arrived, Jackson was not to be denied. He received 647,292 popular votes to Adams' 507,730, but in the Electoral College the margin was wide: Jackson 178, Adams 83.

Jackson's inauguration attracted an astonishingly large crowd of ordinary people, office seekers, and personal friends Daniel Webster, who witnessed the spectacle, wrote, "I never saw anything like it before. Persons have come five hundred miles to see General Jackson, and they really seem to think that the country is rescued from some dreadful danger." An anti-Jackson man declared, "To us, who had witnessed the quiet and orderly period of the Adams Administration, it seemed as if half the nation had rushed at once into the capital. It was like the inundation of the northern barbarians into Rome...."

Little did the patrician class and the politicians realize that a new day had dawned. Jackson used the powers of his office to introduce what became known as the "spoils system"—rewarding with political appointments those who had supported him and his party. These men were expected to contribute ten percent of their salaries to party coffers, as well as work directly for the party. The result was a strong Democratic Party.

The Democratic Party, as well as the Whig Party which rose in opposition by 1832, was forced to be more responsive to popular wishes. The strongest evidence of this acknowledgment of the power of the common man was in the new method of selecting presidential candidates. Until 1824 candidates were nominated by a caucus of important political figures in Congress. In 1828, a vacuum existing, candidates were nominated by state legislatures, state nominating conventions, and political conferences. The national nominating convention, which yet is used, was first used by the Anti-Masonic Party, a minor organization, in 1831 when it selected William Wirt; in 1832 the Democrats were forced to follow suit. The people no longer would allow presidential candidates to be selected by a few men. Nor would they allow members of the Electoral College to be chosen by state legislatures; the process of direct election of electors, already underway in the 1820s, accelerated until by 1840 only South Carolina still selected electors in the legislature.

The growth of the political party, the direct election of members of the Electoral College, and universal adult, white, male suffrage brought great changes to politics, especially in the area of organization. Getting the maximum number of voters to the polls required state, county, and even precinct organization. And the party that won had to reward its faithful workers, so it needed to control the presidency, Congress, and state and local offices. The Democratic Party proved most effective at this task of organization and would dominate national politics for thirty-two years (1828-1860) despite wars, depressions, and scandals.

In these thirty-two years occurred yet more dramatic changes. Cities grew rapidly; immigration pushed the population of the United States upward from 12,860,692 in 1830 to 31,443,321 in 1860; industrialization proceeded at a dizzy pace, spurred by myriad inventions, the growth of corporate financing, and an expanded market; transportation for goods and people was facilitated by a growing network of railroads; a dozen more states were added to the Union; while a growing sectional strife was threatening to rend the country apart. Southerners were not participating in the new developments in industry. Their society had remained relatively static—an agricultural society based on slave labor, one dependent upon the North for manufactured goods, insurance, banking, and transportation. Often in debt to Northerners, these Southerners were alarmed at the growing power of the national government, and insisted that the rights of state governments and the people be respected.

Probably a compromise could have been arranged between North and South, one acceptable to both sides, had not the issue been clouded by a growing clamor by many Northerners that slavery be ended. These abolitionists declared that slavery was morally wrong in a country whose philosophy was "All men are created equal." A new political party arose to answer this need, the Republican Party, and in 1860 it elected its candidate for President, Abraham Lincoln with thirty-nine percent of the popular vote and a sectional vote in the Electoral College. Leaders in the Southern states reacted by calling for secession from the Union, and, one by one, eleven states withdrew to form the Confederate States of America. This incipient country would have a national government close to that outlined in the Articles of Confederation.

For four terrible years civil war raged, bringing an end to hundreds of thousands of lives and the expenditure of millions of dollars. Early in the conflict President Lincoln, hoping to cause trouble behind Southern lines, issued his Emancipation Proclamation. Dated September 22, 1862, but to take effect the following January 1, it stipulated that all slaves in the area still in rebellion were free. Of course, this did not affect those slaves in the loyal border states. Many abolitionists were jubilant at the Emancipation Proclamation, but opposition to the plan came from many Northerners unhappy at having to fight a war on behalf of Southern slaves. That fall the Democrats carried many states, even Lincoln's Illinois, but they did not gain control of Congress. Final emancipation of the slaves did not come legally until the thirteenth amendment was ratified; Congress passed this

Abraham Lincoln

measure, which clearly outlaws slavery or involuntary servitude except in punishment for a crime, on February 1, 1865, and by December 18 that year it had been accepted by twenty-seven states.

When the Civil War drew to a close—and Abraham Lincoln was assassinated—Congress fell under the dominance of a group known as Radical Republicans. Their aim was to punish the South for secession by refusing these states readmission to the Union until full civil and political rights had been extended to the freed slaves, and to perpetuate Radical Republican rule in Washington. In these desires they were frustrated by President Andrew Johnson, who had succeeded the dead Lincoln to the presidency. This contest came to a head in February of 1866 when Johnson vetoed a bill extending the life of a Reconstruction bureau, one which he considered an unconstitutional invasion of states' rights. Enraged, the Radicals responded by passing the Civil Rights Bill which extended American citizenship to the ex-slaves. Johnson likewise vetoed this bill on constitutional grounds, but it passed over his veto.

The Radicals decided to put the principles of the Civil Rights Bill into the Constitution by means of an amendment. This one, the fourteenth, passed Congress on June 16, 1866, and conferred national and state citizenship on "All persons born or naturalized in the United States"; moreover, it declared that "No state shall make or enforce any law which shall abridge the privileges or immunities of citizens of the United States" nor deprive them of their life, liberty, and property "without due process of law," and it struck down the old three-fifths compromise by stating that representation in Congress was to be based on the "whole number of persons in each State, excluding Indians not taxed." These Radical Congressmen then insured that the amendment would be ratified by forcing any Southern state wanting back into the Union to accept it as a condition of reentry; without this provision the amendment never would have been ratified, for many Northern states rejected it. On July 28, 1868, this amendment became part of the Constitution.

Shortly after the election of 1868, wherein the Republicans won only because of Southern black votes, the

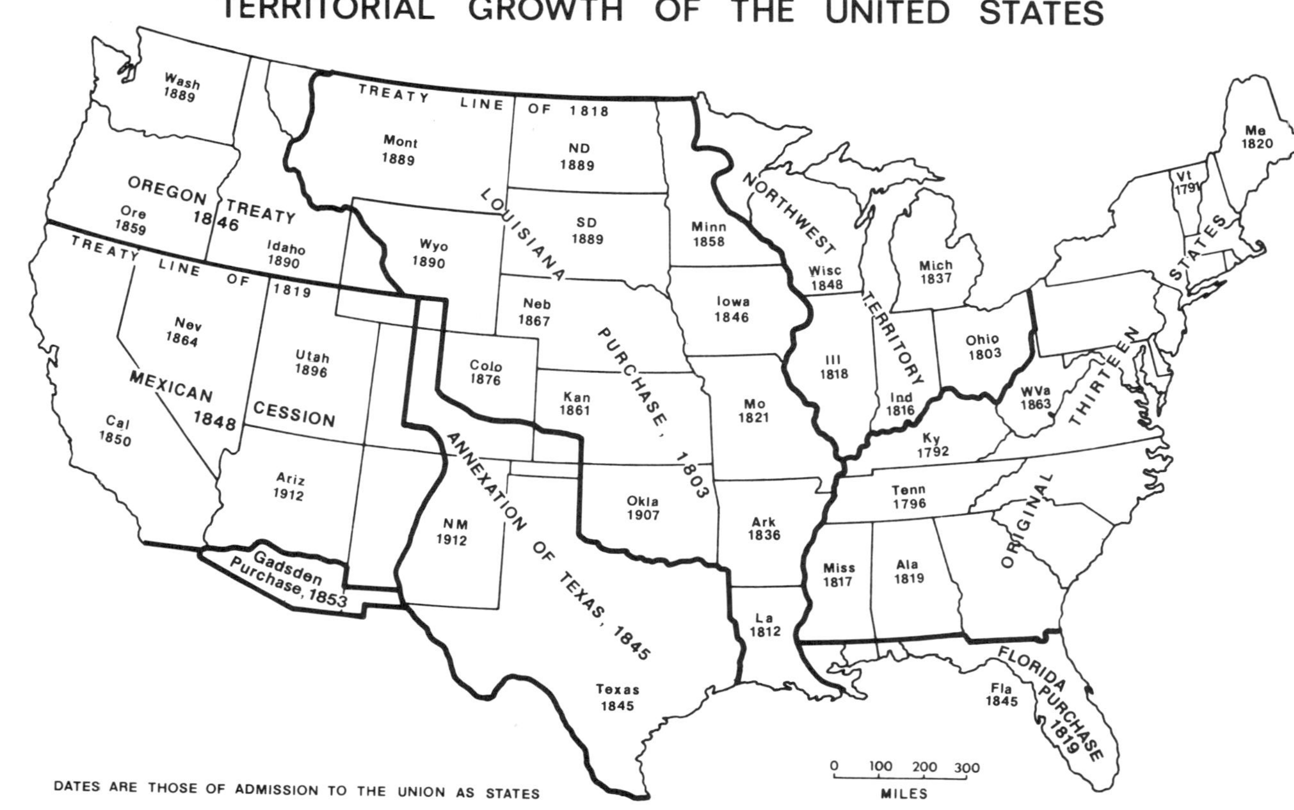

TERRITORIAL GROWTH OF THE UNITED STATES
Wash 1889
OREGON TREATY 1846
Ore 1859
TREATY LINE OF 1819
Nev 1864
MEXICAN CESSION 1848
Cal 1850
Idaho 1890
Ariz 1912
Utah 1896
Gadsden Purchase, 1853
NM 1912
TREATY LINE OF 1818
Mont 1889
ND 1889
LOUISIANA
Wyo 1890
SD 1889
Minn 1858
Neb 1867
Colo 1876
Kan 1861
PURCHASE, 1803
Iowa 1846
Mo 1821
ANNEXATION OF TEXAS, 1845
Okla 1907
Ark 1836
Texas 1845
La 1812
Miss 1817
NORTHWEST
Wisc 1848
TERRITORY
Mich 1837
Ill 1818
Ind 1816
Ohio 1803
WVa 1863
Ky 1792
Tenn 1796
Ala 1819
ORIGINAL THIRTEEN STATES
Me 1820
Vt 1791
FLORIDA PURCHASE 1819
Fla 1845
DATES ARE THOSE OF ADMISSION TO THE UNION AS STATES
0 100 200 300
MILES
152

Radicals decided to incorporate Negro suffrage into the
Constitution. On February 27, 1869, Congress passed and
sent the fifteenth amendment to the states; this stated in
blunt terms that no American citizen could be denied the vote
on the basis of "race, color, or previous condition of
servitude." Those Southern states still under reconstruction
governments were required to ratify this amendment as part
of the condition for reentry into the Union, and on March 30,
1870, Congress announced that this amendment had become
part of the Constitution. Legally thereafter all adult males in
the United States had the vote. But with the addition of these
three amendments the reforming spirit seemed to be spent,
and five decades would pass before additional changes would
be made.

In those five decades the United States changed yet
again. The population jumped from 31,443,321 in 1860 to
91,972,266 in 1910 as tens of millions of immigrants moved
to America to participate in the dream of equality. Here they
and the native citizens found cities growing at an astonishing
rate, manufacturing increasing until it became the major
source of employment, the percentage of people engaged in
farming decreasing steadily until it became a minor source
of employment, new states added to the Union so that by
February 14, 1912, there were forty-eight states, and
inventions by the hundreds changing the way Americans
lived. Telephones, electricity, and automobiles became
commonplace, while airplanes could be seen occasionally.
During this same period the national government came
increasingly into the hands of special interest groups of
businessmen, the rich, and politicians—or so it seemed to
ordinary working people. The reaction came in the last
decades of the nineteenth century as the laborers of America
sought an interest in and a right to a fair share of the wealth
they created.

Prior to the Civil War there had been some attempts to
form labor unions to secure better working conditions and
greater pay for workers, but these had been stifled by the
panics of 1837 and 1857. During the Civil War and
immediately afterward, the United States was industrialized
at a dizzy pace, and the "Captains of Industry" who emerged

were intent on securing the maximum amount of production from their laborers at the least possible pay. In fact, these men would have been considered "brutish and selfish" by the political philosophers of the Age of the Enlightenment who had talked of man in a state of nature, for working conditions in this era were appalling. Between 1865 and 1900 the basic wage changed little: $1.50 for a ten-hour day. Children as young as ten were working the same hours, but for less pay. Industrial accidents were common, for there were few laws requiring safety devices. Periodic layoffs from work were common during the cyclic readjustments in the economy, but unrestricted immigration provided a source of cheap labor and helped kill many strikes that were attempted. Gradually this seething mass of humanity that toiled in the factories began to want some redefinition of the concept of property in order that they might share more equally.

And for a time it seemed that this change might come either legislatively or through judicial order. One early target of those who felt abused was the railroads, and in 1870 Illinois responded to popular demands by passing a law creating a commission which had the power to regulate freight rates. Railroad officials fought this law all the way to the Supreme Court, but in the case *Munn v. Illinois* the Court in 1877 ruled that railroads were clothed with a public interest and therefore subject to public regulation. This judicial ruling, in effect, drastically changed the American concept of property; previously all property was regarded as private and subject only to individual regulation, but after this decision property was considered subject to legislative regulation when the public good was involved. Nine years later the Supreme Court reversed itself in the case *Wabash, St. Louis and Pacific Railroad v. Illinois* by ruling that no state could regulate an enterprise involved in interstate commerce, for that power could be exercised only "by the Congress of the United States under the commerce clause of the Constitution." This decision made inevitable a federal regulatory act for the railroads, and one came on February 4, 1887. This Interstate Commerce Act created an Interstate Commerce Commission with power to enforce rates that were "reasonable and just" and which provided fines and imprisonment for corporations and their agents who violated federal laws.

Thus by legislative and judicial action, the United States had recognized that the property of certain corporations and individuals was tinged with a public interest and thus subject to regulation. Extending that concept to provide that labor should get a greater share of the "property" of industrialists seemed the next step, and labor unions began agitation in that direction.

Because the individual was weak and powerless in negotiating with a giant corporation, workers began organizing into unions. The first of these in the post-Civil War period was the National Labor Union, founded in Baltimore in 1866. By 1868 it claimed 600,000 members, but was oriented toward political—rather than economic—action, and failed to survive the Panic of 1873.

Equally impractical was the Noble and Holy Order of the Knights of Labor, organized in 1869 in Philadelphia. Its aims were "to secure to the toilers a proper share of the wealth they create." One method they employed was to organize cooperatives to produce and distribute goods. By early 1886 this union had sufficient success to attract more than 700,000 members, and the leadership planned a "May Day Rally" in Chicago that year to demonstrate in favor of the eight-hour working day. The choice of cities proved unfortunate, for in Chicago a bitter strike was in progress against the McCormick Harvester Company. At the rally in Haymarket Square on May 3, a bomb was thrown at the police; one officer was killed and several were injured by the explosion. In the subsequent riot an additional seven policemen were killed along with four civilians, and hundreds were injured.

The violence of the Haymarket demonstration turned public opinion against the Knights of Labor, and the organization died quickly. The American public always has turned against any organization or group employing violence against life and property; violence has seemed somehow un-American, and has never been tolerated as a means of achieving any goals, however noble, for there have been peaceful and institutionalized means of securing change.

Next to rise was a different type of union, the business

An engraving of the police firing on the anarchists at Haymarket Square in Chicago

Contemporary print of the events during the Homestead Strike
(engraved by Kurz & Allison Art Studio)

union or craft union. These then were organized into the American Federation of Labor in 1886 by Samuel Gompers, a New York cigar maker. But the growth of this union was slow because of additional violence. In 1892 the Carnegie Steel Company arbitrarily cut wages, whereupon the A. F. of L. announced a strike. Henry C. Frick, the president of the company, responded with a lockout, and hired three hundred Pinkerton detectives to protect company property at Homestead, Pennsylvania. The Pinkerton men came to the plant on barges, and the workers, knowing the schedule, met them at the docks with dynamite and guns on July 6. In the pitched battle that followed, three guards and ten workers died. Frick thereupon asked for protection by the state militia and received it, while public opinion, at first sympathetic to the strikers, turned against them. Slowly the workers drifted back to their jobs, their cause lost. In fact, the violence of Haymarket and Homestead cost labor dearly; more than forty years would pass before the public would forget the violence and Congress would enact legislation protecting the rights of unions.

Yet the frustrations of the workers, when joined with those of the farmers and other segments of the population, would bring change. In the last decade of the nineteenth and first two decades of the twentieth centuries, they were joined by intellectuals who considered reform fashionable, and out of this came the period known as the Progressive Era. Other progressives included the newly emerging middle class: professional men such as lawyers not profiting from the large corporations; ministers and religious leaders who sensed their influence was slipping into the hands of businessmen; educators tired of training technicians; small businessmen who were being squeezed out by the giant corporations; and women who wanted the vote and the prohibition of the sale of alcoholic beverages.

The progressive aims were diverse. Some segments of the movement wanted to reform the cities; at this time the municipal governments of many cities were notoriously corrupt and were not meeting fire, sanitation, police, school, and recreational needs of their inhabitants. Other progressives were angry at the political machines at the state and local level, machines which, in large measure, endured to help the immigrants adjust to life in America in return for votes. Other progressives demanded that the captains of industry have a social conscience. These progressives favored regulation of large industries and safety legislation to control industry. Sometimes one segment of the progressive movement would collapse, or parts of the movement would be working in opposition to yet other parts, but occasionally all segments would unite to fight for a common cause. The voting strength of the progressive movement was the white-collar workers whose only method of economic protest was their ballots, for they did not have trade unions or trade associations. Leadership came from this same urban middle class, usually college educated and frequently self-employed native-born Protestants.

Many of the demands of the progressives were met during the first decade of the twentieth century. At the state and national level the progressives legislated safety and sanitation codes in industry, child labor laws curbing many abuses, workmen's compensation laws, women's labor laws, prison reform, and regulation of big business through anti-trust legislation. Yet their major demands were unfulfilled: a graduated income tax, direct election of United States Senators rather than appointment by state legislatures, national prohibition, and women's suffrage.

Once again the process for achieving the demands of the public was amending the Constitution. The first of the so-called progressive amendments concerned the graduated income tax. During the Civil War and immediately afterward the federal government had secured substantial revenue from an income tax on individuals, but that law was allowed to lapse. In 1893 the government again turned to the income tax to raise funds; however, the Supreme Court ruled that such a tax was unconstitutional because it was a direct tax not apportioned on the basis of population (although the Supreme Court had upheld the income tax during the Civil War). On July 12, 1909, at the urging of progressives, Congress responded by submitting the sixteenth amendment to the states; this stated bluntly, "The Congress shall have power to lay and collect taxes on income, from whatever source derived, without apportionment among the several states, and without regard to any census or enumeration." The amendment finally was ratified by the necessary thirty-six states on February 25, 1913.

As applied by the federal government, the income tax law has been used to redistribute the wealth. The first rate seemed ridiculously high: one percent on income above four thousand dollars a year, rising another percent on income over twenty thousand dollars a year to a total of six percent on income above $500,000 per year.

The method prescribed by the Constitution for electing national Senators was similar to that for selecting a President—by indirect means; the founding fathers in Philadelphia clearly did not trust popular voting. For the president the method was the Electoral College; Senators were to be chosen by state legislatures. However, the arrival of universal adult, male suffrage was soon followed by a demand that the people should elect their Senators directly. When the progressive era arrived, the demand grew louder— and between 1893 and 1902 the House of Representatives on five occasions voted such a resolution. But the Senate failed to act on these. Conservatives in the Senate and in the nation argued against such an amendment, saying that the upper house of Congress should be more deliberative and not responsive to the immediate whims of the people.

By 1912, however, the people were not to be denied, and on May 16 that year Congress submitted the seventeenth amendment to the states for their decision. Ratification took just one year and fifteen days; on May 31, 1913, Congress announced that the necessary three-fourths of the states had accepted the amendment—and both houses of the national legislative body thereafter had to court the favor of the voters at home.

In the two decades, 1897-1917, the progressive spirit swept much of America. The era produced much legislation designed to enoble mankind and change human nature. Some of these reforms definitely were needed. Some were beneficial. Some proved ridiculous, for people remained themselves: corruption continued, while sloth and laziness were not eliminated. Possibly the most noble of these attempts—as well as the most violated—was national

A Currier and Ives print depicting "Womans Holy War, Grand Charge on the Enemy's Works"

prohibition. For three-quarters of a century prior to World War I there were reformers seeking to be rid of "demon rum." A splinter political organization, the Prohibition Party, began offering a presidential candidate in every election beginning in 1872. Although the prohibitionists had little national success, they did achieve it in some local areas; for example, the state of Maine voted itself dry in 1842. With the coming of World War I, however, the prohibitionists began arguing that drying the country would save badly needed grain for the war effort. In addition, many brewers were of German origin, which made prohibition seem patriotic. Congress agreed by sending the eighteenth amendment to the states on December 3, 1917. The state legislatures outdid themselves in seeking to show their patriotic fervor by adopting the amendment, and it was added to the Constitution on January 29, 1919, to take effect one year later. The Volstead Act of October 28, 1919, defined as intoxicating any beverage with more than one-half percent alcohol in it, and made the Internal Revenue Service responsible for enforcing the measure; the Volstead Act also prohibited the manufacture, sale, or transport of such beverages in interstate commerce. Perhaps no law in American history was violated so flagrantly—which shows that occasionally, when the drive to realize the American ideal moves so far that it violates the rights of private citizens, the people disregard the law. Finally the popular will asserted itself, and the twenty-first amendment was added to the Constitution on December 5, 1933; this repealed the prohibition amendment and restored the freedom of the individual with regard to alcoholic beverages.

The fourth—and final—progressive amendment dealt with securing the vote for women. Since 1848, when women met to demand their rights at the Seneca Falls Convention, demands had been made by many individuals and organizations for social, economic, and political equality for females. After the Civil War, national leaders, such as Susan B. Anthony, Elizabeth Cady Stanton, Julia Ward Howe, and Lucy Stone, kept agitating for the goal through speeches, petitions, conventions, and articles, bombarding Congress and prominent politicians with their repeated calls. Everywhere,

(From the top clockwise) Lucretia Mott, E. Cady Stanton, Mary A. Livermore, Lydia Maria Child, Susan B. Anthony, Grace Greenwood, and (center Anna E. Dickinson—all active in the woman's rights movement in the post-Civil War era

however, they met indifference and amused tolerance; even an appeal to the Supreme Court in 1875 *(Minor v. Happersett)* brought rejection, for the court ruled that the vote was not a privilege of citizenship.

When women's clubs began forming in the last quarter of the nineteenth century—and then joined with the militant organizations of feminists—they were able to secure the vote in some states: Wyoming, Colorado, Idaho, and Utah; in fact, by 1912 nine states (all in the West) had granted **females the** right to vote. During World War I women were called upon to undertake many tasks previously reserved for males, and this gave them an additional argument for the right to vote—this and the oft-made statement that women would not be sufficiently gullible to vote for rascally politicians and thus would bring about better government. On June 4, 1919, Congress responded by passing the nineteenth amendment, whereupon women turned their attention to various state legislatures; by August 26, 1920, they had the necessary votes. No longer could the franchise "be denied or abridged by the United States or by any State on account of sex."

During the forty years after universal adult suffrage was achieved, America underwent change of almost unimaginable proportions. The population increased from 105,710,620 in 1920 to 179,323,175 (including the two new states of Hawaii and Alaska, which had been added). Another major conflict, World War II, had been fought, during which the atomic age arrived and the United States clearly became the major power of the world. The American manufacturing capacity grew rapidly in the 1920s, then withered during the Great Depression of 1929-1941, only to boom during World War II to the point where it supplied much of the free world with goods. The middle class expanded rapidly in this period, coming to expect one—and then two—cars, several radio sets, television, and myriad labor-saving appliances. A national highway system brought trucking companies to compete with the railroads in transporting the nation's goods to market, and then the jet age brought air freight to perform the service even faster. In short, the middle class expanded rapidly as far more people escaped from poverty through hard work.

These gains were not made without government help, however, and most of this came during the administration of President Franklin D. Roosevelt. A patrician liberal from New York, he came to office during the depth of the Great Depression with the backing of organized labor. He repaid the leaders of labor unions for their support by helping secure passage of the National Labor Relations Act (or Wagner Act) in 1935. This guaranteed organized labor the right to bargain collectively and outlawed unfair practices against unions. Under the encouragement of a pro-union and anti-business National Labor Relations Board, unions in the decades that followed repeatedly struck selected industries and gained substantial raises for their employees. Roosevelt followed this gain for workers with the Fair Labor Standards Act of 1938; this set a minimum wage of twenty-five cents per hour (raised frequently in the years since) and set maximum working hours in industries engaged in interstate commerce at forty-four per week. In addition, it provided for time-and-a-half pay for overtime work, and forbade child labor on products shipped in interstate commerce. Labor finally had achieved the goals which it had sought in the 1880s and 1890s, but which had been lost then through violence.

These same workers also secured from Roosevelt yet other benefits—which, in effect, constituted a newer definition of property. In his first administration the President recommended and Congress enacted legislation authorizing federal jobs for the out-of-work; this included the Tennessee Valley Authority, which constructed dams and power plants, and the Civil Works Administration, which evolved into the Works Progress Administration (WPA) that hired 2,500,000 by 1935 to lay sidewalks, rake leaves, paint murals on post office walls, and write local history. Through such action the President was construing property to mean the right of every able-bodied American to have a job, even if it must be provided by the national government.

This broadening of the concept of property for individuals was matched by a narrowing of the concept of corporate property. The Roosevelt administration asked for and received from Congress authority to create regulatory agencies; the Securities and Exchange Commission, for the

stock market, the Federal Communications Commission for
interstate and foreign communication, and the Federal
Housing Administration to insure homes and build new ones.

Also, the concept of property was extended during the
Roosevelt years to include the rights of ordinary citizens to
have unemployment compensation, old age pensions, and
security for widows and orphans. This was accomplished by
the Social Security Act of 1935 and provided for money to be
paid to the unemployed through a federal-state system, for a
regular monthly pension to those past age sixty-five, and for
the same regular monthly payment to the blind, crippled,
dependent children, and widows, all financed by a payroll tax
on both employer and employee.

To protect earnings of workers, the Roosevelt
administration secured passage through Congress of the
Glass-Steagall Banking Reform Act which created the Federal
Deposit Insurance Corporation. The FDIC insured individual
deposits to a maximum of $5000 so that workers no longer
would have to worry about losing their savings through bank
failure, a problem that had plagued citizens since the days of
Andrew Jackson.

The emerging middle class, including high-paid laborers,
sent their children to college in increasing numbers in the
years following World War II. The resulting growth in college
enrollments raised the educational level of the nation; this, in
turn, allowed business to make yet more technological gains,
farmers to become so productive that only eight percent of
the population would be engaged in agriculture, and cities to
grow dramatically.

Such drastic change was not without accompanying
problems. The discovery of atomic energy also meant that the
world was under the threat of nuclear holocaust. Rivalry
between the United States and Russia produced the "Cold
War" which threatened to become a hot war—and did in
Korea in 1950-1953 and again in Viet Nam in the mid-1960s.
Industrial pollution and urban blight, along with air pollution
(smog), seemed about to change the balance of nature, while
Americans suddenly became aware that their natural
resources were not going to last forever.

This era also saw the addition of two housekeeping

amendments to the Constitution: the twentieth (1933) which changed the date for inaugurating a President to January 20 and the beginning of a new Congress to January 3; and the twenty-second (1951) which restricted a President to only two terms in office. Finally, just at the end of this period, yet another amendment was added to the Constitution, this one coming after the assassination of President John F. Kennedy. The twenty-fifth amendment, passed by Congress in July 1965 and ratified in February 1967, provided that in cases where the President was removed or resigned, the Vice-President would become President (the original wording of the Constitution had provided that "the powers and duties" of the President would devolve upon the Vice-President through death, removal, or resignation; however, the Constitution did not state that the Vice-President in such cases would be named "President").

One other amendment came during this period, the twenty-third. More than a mere housekeeping addition, this one extended to the people of the District of Columbia the right to choose electors for President and Vice-President. However, the District can never have "more [electors] than the least populous State." This amendment remedied a defect in the Constitution, one not anticipated by the founding fathers: the residents of the seat of government of this representative democracy had no say until the addition of this amendment in 1961 in the selection of the chief executive of the nation.

By the mid-1960s the dramatic changes of the preceding four decades had brought renewed demands for social change. Youths raised under the threat of atomic destruction were demanding an end to war—just as the conflict in Viet Nam was escalating; women, who increasingly were joining the work force, wanted equality in pay and treatment; and minorities, generally at the bottom of the economic ladder, wanted to share in the material goods that American society was producing. Critics of every facet of American society were easy to find: of the environment, of the punishment of criminals, of the draft, which conscripted young men to go to war in Southeast Asia, of the treatment of women, of the failure of minorities to gain equality. Demonstrations

escalated into riots, peaceful protest saw the civil rights of
opponents crushed, and the sanctity of property was widely
violated—even with bombs.

Some of the demands of society for redress could be met
through Congressional legislation: the draft was ended,
pollution standards were adopted for industry and
automobiles, and civil rights legislation was passed to
guarantee the rights of all citizens of whatever race. Even the
death penalty for all crimes was ended in many states, while
the Supreme Court halted executions as it deliberated
whether capital punishment constituted "cruel and unusual
punishment."

Yet some of the demands of the reformers could not be
met without constitutional change. To prevent Southern
states from using a poll tax as a means of preventing Negroes
from voting, Congress in 1962 sent the twenty-fourth
amendment to the states; this stated that "The right of
citizens of the United States to vote in any primary or other
election" for national officials "shall not be denied or abridged
by the United States or any State by reason of failure to pay
any poll tax or other tax." The necessary states agreed, and
the amendment became part of the Constitution in the
summer of 1964.

The second of these "new progressive" amendments
came in 1971 to appease youngsters, especially the college
radicals. It lowered the voting age to eighteen. A third
amendment is currently being considered by the various
states; it states "Equality of rights under the law shall not be
denied or abridged by the United States or any State on
account of sex," and was passed by Congress to appease
militant feminists—who gained attention for the plight of
women through publicity stunts, confrontations, and
protests. As yet the necessary thirty-eight states have not
endorsed this amendment.

Reformers today still are discussing the possibility of
adding new amendments to accomplish changes which they
feel are needed. For example, since the Supreme Court of the
United States outlawed prayers in the public schools, there
have been many efforts to secure passage of an amendment
making this legal. And in the conflict over the bussing of

school children to achieve racial balance, proponents of one viewpoint or another have discussed the desirability of constitutional change. Such talk proves that the Constitution is a living document, one capable of being changed to meet the requirements of evolving public desires.

Franklin D. Roosevelt

The Bi-Centennial of the Miracle

Among historians there are those who believe in the cyclical theory of history—that is, that history repeats itself endlessly. Those who subscribe to this theory point out that American history divides itself into cycles of approximately forty-year periods. When the Bill of Rights was added to the Constitution in 1790-1791, the participants in government tended to be only wealthy white males. There followed a period of about forty years in which only two amendments were added to the Constitution to perfect slight flaws. Then, in the "Age of Jackson," great changes were wrought— through legislation rather than constitutional amendments— to produce universal adult, white, male suffrage. This was in keeping with the social and economic changes occurring since the days when the present government came into existence. There followed another period of some thirty-five to forty years in which additional changes occurred, and the Reconstruction amendments were added to enfranchise adult Negro males.

Another quiet period—in the legal, constitutional sense— followed, during which there were great social and economic changes. Finally, in the period 1913 to 1920, the progressive amendments were added to the Constitution to make that document more truly reflect popular desires: the income tax, direct election of United States Senators, prohibition, and the enfranchisement of adult females.

After 1920 there followed another time of great economic and social change in America, one wherein demands for reform were met through legislative change. There were several amendments to the Constitution of a "housekeeping" nature: ending the lame-duck session of Congress by moving forward the date when new Congresses are inaugurated, limiting the President to two terms in office, allowing the residents of the District of Columbia to be represented in the Electoral College, and providing for the naming of a new Vice-President upon the death, resignation, or removal of the President. In addition, the nation repealed prohibition through constitutional amendment when this progressive measure no longer suited the desires of the people.

Then in the 1960s and 1970s came more changes in the Constitution to reflect new public attitudes: citizens no longer could be prevented from voting because of failure to pay a poll tax or any other tax, and the legal age at which adults could vote was reduced to eighteen. The third of these new progressive amendments, equal rights under the law for females, has yet to secure the necessary ratification by three-quarters of the states.

Believers in the cyclical theory of history might argue that the country now will have another forty or so years of tranquility, at least in a constitutional sense. However, other historians believe that events move not in cycles but in a linear direction; the proponents of this theory argue that each nation seeks to achieve a position in the middle of the road to attain its pragmatic ends. In short, they believe that moderation governs the affairs of nations, that extremes in any direction bring a reaction forcing a return to moderation.

Still others who gaze into the crystal ball of the past and try to predict the future course of events belong to what is known as the "consensus school." They believe that in any nation there is a middle class of people who dictate what the philosophy of that nation is to be—and that in the United States the middle class always has stood for the sanctity of private property; change has come as the middle class has shifted its view of what constitutes private property. The "archtype school" of historians has replied that each culture, each nation, at its moment of creation has a different pattern, but that all are evolving toward the same goal; however, they argue that no one knows what the eventual human destiny is to be.

Many other schools of history have evolved, even one that states that human—and national—events move by random chance and that the future is unpredictable because extraordinary men arise from time to time and influence events in peculiar ways.

Whatever the future holds for the United States, one thing is clear: running through the fabric of our history is a bright, clear thread which boldly asserts that the true ancestors of the American government were not men, but the idea and the ideal that the blessings of society should be open to all. That idea and ideal were a product of the Enlightenment, the colonial experience, and the frustrations of separation from England. The essence of Americanism is that the citizens of the country tried to establish a more perfect union which would guarantee domestic tranquility but which also would guarantee maximum freedom to all. The founding fathers provided this philosophy, along with a constitutional framework and a representative government, which allowed change to come in legal ways. In the 1770s and 1780s government was in the hands of the few, with only adult, white males owning a specified amount of property and, in some instances, belonging to a specified church allowed to participate in our democracy; by the 1970s, without war, all adult citizens, male and female, black and white, have access to high office and ballot box.

Each of these changes has come "in the fullness of time"—as Americans have come to realize that this or that segment of the population was not a participating member of society or as the population gave a new definition to property. In this sense there has been no one American revolution, but rather a continuing series of revolutions—the only revolution in world history that has lived up to its slogans. The American manifesto of its aspirations—the Declaration of Independence—promised "life, liberty, and the pursuit of happiness," and, thanks to the changes wrought in two hundred years, these have been provided to all Americans. In other nations the revolutionaries promised "peace, land, and bread," but delivered war, collective farms, and famine; or "liberty, equality, and fraternity," but gave tyranny and orders of nobility. These foreign revolutionaries swept into office promising an immediate redistribution of wealth and equality for all citizens, but once entrenched in power they dedicated themselves to staying in control; in short, they turned out one form of repressive government only to replace it with another form of repressive (or reactionary) government.

The founding fathers in America fulfilled the slogans of their revolution by providing a vehicle for controlled, evolutionary change. Always the philosophy behind this new government was more important than the legalistic, written form; in the United States the underlying basis of government has not been words on paper but rather an idea engraved on the hearts of men. Other nations have had constitutions and philosophical statements, some of which contained measured sentences that marched with the cadence of a poetry more elegant than the practical words of the American Constitution. But the governments of those nations have changed regularly because the citizens there believed in men, not an immortal idea. Americans have lived with one Declaration of Independence, one Constitution, one Bill of Rights, plus a few amendments because they have subscribed to the ideals therein, not to this or that politician. These ideas are the true American ancestors, not men.

Perhaps this explains why there was such popular indignation over the events of 1972-1974 now labeled "Watergate." The citizens of other nations wondered why Americans became so incensed when they learned that the President and his close advisors apparently had broken the law. The reason was—and is—that Americans believe that even a President is not above the law. The continuing revolutionary spirit in America rebels at the thought of anyone violating the ideal of the country.

The men who conceived the American government, who drafted its Declaration of Independence and its Constitution, were citizens of affairs and substance, men generally referred to as "conservative." Yet they produced documents truly "liberal" in that these have formed the basis of the most progressive government ever created, one wherein men of merit could rise regardless of their origins and one wherein the powers of the national government were sufficient to

meet the needs of changing times without restricting
individual liberties. The American Revolution did not end in
1783 with a treaty in Paris, nor was it completed in 1787
when the Constitution was drafted, nor yet was it ended in
1789 when the new government was instituted. It continued
in the presidencies of Thomas Jefferson and Andrew Jackson;
Abraham Lincoln caught the spirit of the revolution at
Gettysburg when he spoke of the "new nation, conceived in
Liberty, and dedicated to the proposition that all men are
created equal." Theodore Roosevelt, Woodrow Wilson, and
Franklin Roosevelt carried forward the same theme, as did
laborers fighting for their unions, farmers organizing, and
women marching. All were revolutionaries, for they believed,
as did the men enduring at Valley Forge and the delegates
deliberating in Philadelphia, in a government "of the people,
by the people, and for the people."

Yet all these patriots of yesterday realized that the
phrase, "All men are created equal," did not—and could not—
mean that all Americans would have an equal endowment of
intelligence or that all would have the same amount of
wealth. Rather they were dedicated to the concept that every
American should have the right to life, liberty, and the
pursuit of happiness, and that the attainment of all three of
these depend on individual initiative, individual discipline, and
individual work. Such things cannot—and should not—be
imposed by an authoritarian government on inept,
unmotivated individuals. To do so arbitrarily, even from the
best and noblest of motives, is to go counter to the whole idea
and ideal of America, for such action would deprive people of
control of their own lives, liberty, and pursuit of happiness.

As the United States begins its third century of existence,
every American can celebrate the miracle that is his
birthright. All Americans, no matter what their race or creed
or color or even the date of arrival of their ancestors on these
shores, have been and are a part of the continuing revolution.
No Black American need manufacture a hero out of a man of
cloudy racial background and swear he died in the Boston
Massacre. No American of Spanish ancestry needs to feel
ashamed of the events at the Alamo. There is no necessity for
such things because all Americans of the current generation

are full and equal participants in the miracle that is the United States—provided they believe that "all men are created equal, that all are endowed by their Creator with certain unalienable rights; that among these are life, liberty, and the pursuit of happiness; that, to secure these rights, governments are instituted among men, deriving their just powers from the consent of the governed." All Americans should rededicate themselves to this great idea and ideal. They should forget color lines, minimize their philosophical differences, and pledge again that they are determined to sacrifice, if need be, "our Lives, our Fortunes, and our sacred Honor" to preserve the greatest and noblest experiment in world history. Here their ancestors and they have implemented the highest aspirations of mankind everywhere.

And "in the fullness of time" the revolution continues.

Bibliography

CHAPTER 1

Adams, Charles Francis. Ed., *The Works of John Adams*. 10 vols. Boston: Little, Brown and Company, 1850-1856.

Andrews, Charles M. *The Colonial Background of the American Revolution*. New Haven: Yale University Press, 1931.

Bailyn, Bernard. *The Ideological Origins of the American Revolution*. Cambridge: Belknap Press, 1967.

Boyd, Julian. Ed., *The Papers of Thomas Jefferson*. Princeton: Princeton University Press, 1950.

Leach, Douglas E. *The Northern Colonial Frontier*. New York: Holt, Rinehart and Winston, 1966

CHAPTER 2

Adams, James Truslow. *The Living Jefferson*. New York: Charles Scribner's Sons, 1936.

Becker, Carl Lotus. *The Eve of the Revolution*. New Haven: Yale University Press, 1918.

————. *The Declaration of Independence: A Study in the History of Political Ideas*. New York: Alfred A. Knopf, Inc., 1922.

Bowen, Catherine Drinker. *John Adams and the American Revolution*. Boston: Little, Brown and Company, 1951.

Gipson, Lawrence H. *The Coming of the Revolution*. New York: Harper, 1959.

Jensen, Merrill. *The Founding of a Nation: A History of the American Revolution, 1763-1776*. New York: Oxford University Press, 1968.

Malone, Dumas. *The Story of the Declaration of Independence*. New York: Oxford, 1954.

————. *Thomas Jefferson and His Time*. 4 Vols, Boston: Little, Brown and Company, 1948.

Morgan, Edmund S. *The Birth of the Republic, 1775-1783*. Chicago: University of Chicago Press, 1956.

Smith, C. Page. *John Adams*. New York: Doubleday, 1962.

CHAPTER 3

Alden, John Richard. *The American Revolution: 1775-1783*. New York: Harper, 1954.

Bemis, Samuel Flagg. *The Diplomacy of the American Revolution*. Bloomington, Indiana: Indiana University Press, 1957.

Burnett, Edmund. Ed., *Letters of the Members of the Continental Congress, 1774-1789*. 8 Vols. Gloucester, Massachusetts: Peter Smith, 1963.

Brown, Weldon A. *Empire or Independence, 1774-1783*. Baton Rouge: Louisiana State University Press, 1941.

Ford, Chauncy Worthington. Ed., *The Journals of the Continental Congress, 1774-1789*. 34 vols. Washington, D.C.: G.P.O. 1904-1937.

Miller, John C. *Triumph of Freedom, 1775-1783*. Boston: Little, Brown and Company, *1948*.

Van Tyne, Charles C. *The American Revolution, 1776-1783*. New York: Harper, 1905.

CHAPTER 4

Fiske, John. *The Critical Period of American History*. Boston: Houghton Mifflin Company, 1916.

Henderson, H. James. *Party Politics in the Continental Congress*. New York: McGraw-Hill, 1974.

Jensen, Merrill. *The New Nation*. New York: Alfred A. Knopf, 1950.

__________. *Articles of Confederation*. Madison: University of Wisconsin Press, 1959.

Smith, Jonathan. "Some Features of Shay's Rebellion," *William and Mary Quarterly*, V (1948), 77-109.

CHAPTER 5

Beard, Charles A. *An Economic Interpretation of the Constitution*. New York: MacMillan, 1913.

Brant, Irving. *James Madison*. 6 vols., Indianapolis: Bobbs-Merrill, 1941-1961.

Brown, Robert E. *Charles Beard and the Constitution.* Princeton: Princeton University Press, 1956.

Farrand, Max. *The Framing of the Constitution.* New Haven: Yale University Press, 1913.

————. Ed., *Records of the Federal Convention of 1787.* New Haven: Yale University Press, 1966.

Hunt, Gaillard. Ed., *The Writings of James Madison.* 9 Vols. New York: Putnam, Inc., 1900-1910.

Kurtz, Stephen J. Ed., *The Federalists, Creators and Critics, 1780-1801.* New York: John Riley and Sons, Inc., 1972.

McDonald, Forrest. *We the People: Economic Origins of the Constitution.* Chicago: University of Chicago Press, 1958.

McLaughlin, Andrew. *The Confederation and the Constitution, 1783-1789.* New York: MacMillan, Inc., 1962.

Mitchell, Broadus, and Louise Mitchell. *A Biography of the Constitution, Its Origins, Formation, Adoption, Interpretation.* New York: Oxford University Press, 1964.

Syrett, Harold C., and Jacob E. Cook. Eds., *The Papers of Alexander Hamilton.* New York: Columbia University Press, 1961.

CHAPTER 6

Brant, Irving. *The Bill of Rights, Its Origins and Meanings.* New York: Bobbs-Merrill Company, Inc., 1965.

Hand, Learned. *The Bill of Rights.* Cambridge: Howard University Press, 1958.

Johnson, Allen. *Jefferson and His Colleagues, A Chronicle of the Virginia Dynasty.* New Haven: Yale University Press, 1921. Volume 15 of Yale Chronicles of America Series.

Schwartz, Bernard. Ed., *The Bill of Rights: A Documentary History.* 2 vols., New York: McGraw Hill Book Company, 1971.

CHAPTER 7

Cunliffe, Marcus. *George Washington, Man and Monument.* Boston: Little, Brown, and Company, 1958.

Fitzpatrick, John C. Ed., *Writings of George Washington.* 39 vols., Washington, D.C.: G.P.O., 1931-1950.

Flexner, James Thomas. *George Washington and the New Nation.* Boston: Little, Brown and Company, 1969.

Freeman, Douglas Southadl. *George Washington.* 7 Vols., New York: Scribner's, 1948-1957.

White, Leonard D. *The Federalists, A Study in Administrative History, 1789-1801.* New York: MacMillan Company, 1948.

CHAPTER 8

Barnes, William R. *The Supreme Court Issue and the Constitution.* New York: Barnes and Noble, Inc., 1937.

Bassett, John Spencer. *The Life of Andrew Jackson.* New York: MacMillan Company, 1916.

Blum, Albert A. *A History of the American Labor Movement.* Washington, D.C.: American Historical Association, 1972.

Dulles, Foster Rhea. *Labor in America, A History.* New York: Thomas Y. Crowell Co., 1949.

Fawcett, Dame Millicent. *Women's Suffrage, A Short History of a Great Movement.* New York: Source Book Press, 1970.

Flack, Horace E. *The Adoption of the Fourteenth Amendment.* Baltimore: Johns Hopkins Press, 1908.

Gillette, William. *The Right to Vote: Politics and the Passage of the Fifteenth Amendment,* Baltimore: Johns Hopkins Press, 1965.

Herling, John. *Labor Unions in America.* Washington: R. B. Luce, 1964.

Hibbard, Benjamin H. *A History of the Public Land Policies.* Madison: University of Wisconsin, 1965.

James, Joseph B. *The Framing of the Fourteenth Amendment.* Urbana: University of Illinois Press, 1956.

James, Marquis. *Andrew Jackson.* 2 Vols., New York: Bobbs-Merrill Co., 1933-1937.

Murphy, Paul L. *The Constitution in Crisis Times, 1918-1969.* New York: Harper and Row, 1971.

Paulson, Ross E. *Women's Suffrage and Prohibition: A Comparative Study of Equality and Social Control.* Glenville, Illinois: Scott, Foresman, 1973.

Rottschaefer, Henry. *The Constitution and Socio-Economic Change.* Ann Arbor, Michigan: University of Michigan Law School, 1948.

Schlesinger, Arthur M. *The Age of Jackson.* Boston: Little, Brown and Company, 1945.

————. *The Age of Roosevelt.* 4 vols., Boston: Houghton Mifflin, 1957.

Shaw, Robert. Ed., *Andrew Jackson, 1767-1845: Chronology, Documents, Bibliographical Aids.* Dobbs Ferry, New York: Oceana Publications, 1969.

Vose, Clement. *Constitutional Change: Amendment Politics and Supreme Court Litigation Since 1900.* Lexington, Massachusetts: Lexington Books, 1972.

White, Leonard. *The Jeffersonians, A Study in Administrative History, 1801-1829.* New York: MacMillan Company, 1950.

————. *The Jacksonians, A Study in Administrative History, 1829-1861.* New York: MacMillan Company, 1954.

————. *The Republican Era, A Study in Administrative History, 1869-1901.* New York: MacMillan Company, 1958.

CHAPTER 9

Revel, Jean-Francois. *Without Marx or Jesus: The New American Revolution Has Begun.* New York: Doubleday, 1971.

Index